Thriving In Higher Education Careers

A. Yvette Myrick, Ed.D. & Estelle M. Young, Ph.D.

outskirts
press

Acknowledgements

We are very grateful for the assistance we received from James Allen Myrick (book cover) and Crystal Carpenter (formatting, logistics, researcher, and much more). Their conscientious and thoughtful efforts helped us complete this book.

Table of Contents

Thriving in Higher Education Careers

Welcome to **Thriving in Higher Education Careers**. The authors, Drs. A. Yvette Myrick and Estelle Young, believe that public service is a noble calling. It offers an opportunity to make a lasting and profound impact on individual lives and to improve the policies and programs that affect many people. We found our passion in public service through working in higher education. When we embarked on our careers more than 20 years ago, we were well aware of and willing to make the sacrifices necessary to put in the long hours, live on the lower pay compared to the private sector, and work in environments with limited resources.

But we were often surprised by and not prepared for some of the challenges of maintaining a meaningful career in higher education. We wrote this book to share the lessons we have learned firsthand, by observing others and through research, to meet those challenges. By sharing these lessons, we hope to help you prepare for challenges, so that you can respond to them proactively and achieve the impact you desire, while maintaining the optimistic and positive attitude that attracted you to public service in the first place.

We hope this book will serve as a resource for people who are contemplating a career in higher education, those that desire to excel in current positions, or those that desire to navigate to other positions in higher education. The book includes tips, informational resources, questions for reflection, and spotlights on professionals whose practices serve as an inspiration. We selected tips that are easy to adopt and implement, low or no cost, and effective. There is also a section for journal writing during the higher education journey. We hope this book is equally useful to both individuals and groups as a part of professional development activities or course instruction.

1

Collaborating and Networking Are Necessary

Introduction

WE ENTER OUR careers in higher education eager to translate our commitment into action. We dive in—designing our courses and joining committees—to contribute to institution building. After putting in many extra hours of hard work, we can get frustrated when we look around and see our students or colleagues not contributing their share. This chapter covers areas of potential collaboration and networking with positive people to facilitate a positive experience with desired outcomes.

5 Tips for Effective Collaboration

In higher education, there are many opportunities to collaborate with colleagues, educators at other institutions, partners in the community, and various stakeholders. Sometimes the collaborations involve working with your students on projects, in student activities, or as part of the learning process during their educational journey. Below are tips regarding areas of collaboration that can maximize your skill set and also foster advancement in your higher education career.

Tip 1: Harness Your Students as Collaborators in the Classroom

For many of us, preparing for class means preparing a lesson plan in which we have distilled key points, identified examples, and made comparisons and contrasts. Active and collaborative learning strategies enable your students to take more responsibility for their own learning.[1] Using such strategies does not mean abandoning the lecture entirely, but rather intentionally reducing the amount of time lecturing and increasing the amount of time students spend engaged in active and collaborative learning.

> *"The teacher is of course an artist, but being an artist does not mean that he or she can make the profile, can shape the students. What the educator does in teaching is to make it possible for the students to become themselves."* —Paulo Friere

Tip 2: Create a Structure for Collaboration by Setting Consistent Expectations for Students and Yourself

Identify your core set of *nonnegotiable expectations*, state them clearly, both verbally and in your syllabus, and impose them consistently.[2] Your expectations should encourage your students to aim high and should be expressed in the affirmative (what to do) rather than what not to do.

---

1   https://www.mcgill.ca/tls/teaching/resources/activelearning
2   https://icoblog.wordpress.com/2012/08/31/setting-expectations-in-the-college-classroom

"Life... It tends to respond to our outlook, to shape itself to meet our expectations." —Richard M. DeVos

Tip 3: Collaborate With Others on the Early Alert System

Many institutions have a process through which students with early missteps can be identified early in the semester, the causes identified, and referrals to appropriate resources made. These early alert systems allow students to redirect or redouble their efforts and recover from initial missteps.[3] Participating actively in these systems brings outside resources into your classroom on behalf of the students. By bringing in resources, you will be able to collaborate with people in different departments within and outside your institution that share a common goal of student retention and completion.

"If we can provide even a few months of early warning for just one pandemic, the benefits will outweigh all the time and energy we're devoting. Imagine preventing health crises, not just responding to them." —Nathan Wolfe

Tip 4: Collaborate With Others on a Major Institutional Initiative

Identify a major institutional initiative that aligns with your convictions. Devote some of your service hours to participating in that initiative. You will have an opportunity to support the institution while working on a project that you find meaningful. Then, collaborate with other faculty, staff, partners outside your institution, community leaders, and various stakeholders who share your dedication to plan and implement the institutional initiative.

---

3   https://www.academicimpressions.com/partnering-with-faculty-in-early-alert-a-faculty-perspective/

The final findings of the BEAMS (Building Engagement and Attainment for Minority Students) project, include the recommendation to link BEAMS with a larger campus initiative to ensure success.[4]

"I've always loved the experience of working together with other people toward an artistic goal." —Trey Anastasio

"At times our own light goes out and is rekindled by a spark from another person. Each of us has cause to think with deep gratitude of those who have lighted the flame within us." — Albert Schweitzer

Tip 5: Collaborate With Others on the Institutional Mission

Reflect on your institution's mission and strategic plan. Identify the shared elements and use the mission to shape your teaching and service efforts. Collaborate with other people who share the devotion in fulfilling the institutional mission.

Project DEEP (Documenting Effective Educational Practice) conducted 20 intensive case studies of colleges and universities graduating more students than would be predicted by their entering characteristics. One of the six key conditions noted was a "lived mission." [5]

"Speaking to numerous teachers and nurses, I am consistently struck by the sense of mission they have about their work." — Charles Kennedy

---

4   https://www.aacu.org/publications-research/periodicals/collaborating-learn-learning-collaborate
5   http://nsse.indiana.edu/html/projectdeep.cfm

5 Tips for Networking with Positive People

A positive working experience enhances our productivity and brings joy to our work as higher education professionals. Sometimes as part of our work experience, we need to network with others. The tips below provide some practical and effective tools to create a positive experience for yourself and others during the networking and collaborating process.

The tips draw from two underlying principles.

Principle 1: You Do Not Control Your Environment; Rather, You Control Your Response to that Environment

Steven Covey's *Seven Habits of Highly Effective People*[6] (Covey, 1989) breaks every environment down into two circular components. The larger circle includes every person, situation, or condition that matters to an individual. Covey called it the "circle of concern." The second, smaller circle represents those things under one's direct or indirect control, the "circle of influence."

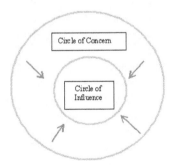

Reactive Focus

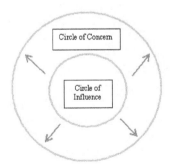

Proactive Focus

6   http://www.depts.ttu.edu/upwardbound/books/the-7-habits-ofhighly-effective-people.pdf

Covey noted that although the environment itself is fixed, the impact of that environment is malleable. When focused on things that are outside your control in your work environment, you take a reactive posture that amplifies the impact of the environment. This phenomenon is depicted in the Reactive Focus circle, with the arrows from the environment reducing the influence of the individual. In contrast, when you take a proactive stance by focusing and acting on aspects within your control, the result is an expansion of the circle of influence over the environment. In the Proactive Focus, the arrows of influence are outward pointing.

Principle 2: Fact—Your Environment Is Full of Positive People

Higher education draws many professionals who enter their careers highly committed to their students, loyal to their institutions, and dedicated to a lifetime of public service. These professionals make up the majority of every college and university. Interactions with people with a shared commitment to profession and optimism about the institution will bolster one's own commitment and optimism. These convictions energize a person and enhance productivity. Heavy workloads and silos characteristic of most institutions make it highly unlikely that all of these professionals know of one another. This situation presents an opportunity for each of us to broaden our circle of influence by expanding our network of positive colleagues; five tips to do just that are outlined below.

Tip 1: Hold on to Your Original Optimism about Public Service

The *beliefs*[7] you held prior to entering your career in higher education are still true. Assume that a meaningful career in higher education in a nurturing environment is not only possible but also within your reach.

---

7   https://www.insidehighered.com/views/2011/08/22/public-service-obligation

"The optimism of a healthy mind is indefatigable." —Margery Allingham

Tip 2: Focus on What You Can Control—Your Interpretation

Notice when your thoughts turn to negative elements in your environment that prevent you from reaching your goals; then intentionally reframe and redirect your thoughts to search for positive elements. More details regarding the steps to cognitive reframing can be found in *Mindtools* and *Psychology Today.*[8]

"God, grant me the serenity to accept the things I cannot change, the courage to change the things I can, and the wisdom to know the difference." —The Serenity Prayer

Tip 3: Identify Positive Role Models Already in Your Circle

These role models are easy to spot. They share fulfilling experiences about the institution and excitement about the future. They rarely complain. The infectious enthusiasm and inspiring initiative of positive role models provide external validation for your reminders to yourself about your positive environment. Medical[9] and psychological[10] studies link coworker support with reduced work stress.

"You should also appreciate the goodness around you, and surround yourself with positive people." —Nadia Comaneci

---

8   https://www.psychologytoday.com/blog/in-practice/201301/cognitive-restructuring

9   https://www.webmd.com/balance/news/20030414/work-support-helps-heart#1

10 http://www.researchersworld.com/vol5/issue2/Paper_08.pdf

Tip 4: Expand Your Positive Circle by Using an Informational Interview Approach

When talking to positive colleagues, ask them to identify other positive colleagues. Worried that this will prove too time consuming? Seek opportunities within your schedule for introductions to new members of your positive network. You could have lunch together during your normal lunch hour or on professional development days. Michele Martin's [11]*The Bamboo Project* provides additional tips and strategies for creating a positive network.

> *"To all the other dreamers out there, don't ever stop or let the world's negativity disenchant you or your spirit. If you surround yourself with love and the right people, anything is possible."*
> —Adam Green

Tip 5: Find Natural Opportunities to Enhance Your Impact by Networking with Positive People

Opportunities for collaboration to reach shared goals naturally emerge from relationships with others who share a professional agenda. Timesaving collaborations can start small. Examples include sharing a grading rubric, swapping useful website links, or exchanging institutional know-how information. Long-term examples include serving jointly on a committee, team teaching a course, or jointly conducting research. These collaborative efforts offer the opportunity to save time and avoid producing duplicate wheels. They help you reach your professional goals and have even greater impact, thereby contributing to your sense of satisfaction and professional wellbeing.

---

11   http://www.michelemmartin.com/thebambooprojectblog/2012/02/the-power-of-positive-peers.html

5 Tips for Dealing with Difficult People

For me, it came as a complete surprise. I knew about the relatively low pay, hard work, and resource challenges of public sector work. But I always assumed I would be surrounded by nothing but joyful, committed, team-spirited, mission-focused colleagues and supervisors. Like many others, I was unprepared for difficult people. With these tips in your toolkit, you will be prepared to face them with ease.

Tip 1: Reframe: Difficult people are teachers.

When interacting, bite your tongue, breathe deeply, and listen for your teachable moment. Finer Minds[12], Simple Mindfulness[13], and Judy Ringer[14] offer ways to create your own teachable moment.

> *"If you really want liberation, if you really want freedom, you will need people around you to be provoking to show you where it is you still have work to do."* – Pema Chodron

> *"In order to become a completely loving person, a flexible person, you have to see where you are hookable."* — Pema Chodron

---

12   http://www.finerminds.com/personal-growth/enemies-or-teachers-what-we-can-learn-from-difficult-people/
13   http://www.simplemindfulness.com/2012/08/10/difficult-people-teachers/
14   http://www.judyringer.com/resources/articles/difficult-people-3-questions-to-help-you-turn-your-tormentors-into-teachers.php

Tip 2: If You Wouldn't Invite them Home for Dinner, Why Let Them Camp in Your Head?

One destructive power of difficult relationships is the amount of time and energy spent ruminating after conversations. Eliminate their power to make your life difficult by reducing rumination[15].

"But it is a melancholy of mine own, compounded of many simples, extracted from many objects, and indeed the sundry contemplation of my travels, which, by often rumination, wraps me in the most humorous sadness." – William Shakespeare.

"It would be much better if I could only stop thinking. Thoughts are the dullest things. Duller than flesh. They stretch out and there's no end to them and they leave a funny taste in the mouth. Then there are words, inside the thoughts, unfinished words, a sketchy sentence which constantly returns...It goes, it goes ... and there's no end to it. It's worse than the rest because I feel responsible and have complicity in it. For example, this sort of painful rumination: I exist, I am the one who keeps it up. I." – Jean-Paul Sartre

Tip 3: Seek Common Ground

Assume there is a kernel of shared wisdom in every conversation and intentionally focus on building on that common ground. The *Psych Central*[16] and *Evoke*[17] blog offer specific strategies to do just this.

---

15   https://irp-cdn.multiscreensite.com/bb2bd6f4/files/uploaded/StopRuminating.pdf
16   http://psychcentral.com/lib/10-rules-for-friendly-fighting-for-couples/2/
17   https://evoke.pro/articles/178/#.VWUQ3c9Viko

"You need people that are willing to talk to the other side, or you're never going to get anything done. You need to be willing to expand your ground. There's always usually a place on issues where you can find common ground." — Amy Klobuchar

"There is not a liberal America and a conservative America - there is the United States of America. There is not a black America and a white America and Latino America and Asian America - there's the United States of America." — Barack Obama

Tip 4: As You Become More Assertive, Their Ability To Be Difficult Diminishes.

There are three steps to assertive communication (Butler and Hope, 2007: 138-9).

1. Identify what you want (be specific and singular).
2. State it clearly and concisely and honestly (stick to the important points).
3. Repeat if necessary either with the same exact words or close paraphrase.

MindTools[18] and the *Skills You Need*[19] blog offer additional strategies for effective and assertive communication.

"I encourage people to remember that 'no' is a complete sentence." – Gavin de Becker

---

18   http://www.mindtools.com/pages/article/Assertiveness.htm
19   http://www.skillsyouneed.com/ps/assertiveness-techniques.html

"There is a fine line between assertiveness and being relaxed."
– Justin Guarini

"To know oneself, one should assert oneself." – Albert Camus

"Ask for what you want and be prepared to get it!" – Maya Angelou

Tip 5: Redefine your objectives.

Ask yourself, is your strategy the only way to reach your goal? Or can you modify it? Letting go is a powerful way to removing the power of others to stand in your way. See Zen Habits[20] or Tiny Budda[21] for inspiration.

"Letting go means to come to the realization that some people are a part of your history, but not a part of your destiny." —— Steve Maraboli

"Holding on is believing that there's only a past; letting go is knowing that there's a future." — Daphne Rose Kingma

---

20   http://zenhabits.net/zen-attachment/
21   http://tinybuddha.com/blog/10-questions-to-ask-yourself-before-giving-up-on-your-dream/

Spotlights – Professionals Who Stay the Course

This section features professionals who have mastered the tips recommended in this book. We hope their stories and strategies inspire you. We start off with one of our favorite strategies, collaboration, featuring our own collaboration as a spotlight.

A.Yvette Myrick

Estelle Young

Effective Collaboration

We met over a decade ago when we collaborated on a project to increase the number of faculty and students participating in an early-alert process to identify students at risk of failure sufficiently early to allow them to redirect or redouble their effort and improve their performance. Over the years, we collaborated on several projects, including a developmental or transitional education learning community, an initiative to foster achievement motivation, and a blog that was a precursor to this book. We collaborate most intensively in different areas: A. Yvette in the classroom and administration and Estelle when working on projects. Our methods are described below. A. Yvette very consciously and intentionally sets consistent expectations and structures her classes with active and collaborative learning. On the first day of class, she solicits expectations from the students of their ideal educational experience in and out of class. Through that activity, the class establishes its own set of mutually agreed upon expectations for a classroom setting most conducive to their learning. The daily cycle of activities follows a predictable routine, thereby providing another avenue for establishing consistent expectations. She introduces the day's material with a story to spark interest or a question to connect to prior knowledge. She briefly reviews and then introduces the day's activity. She organizes the students into intentional groupings, with, for example, students skilled at public speaking being assigned to report for the group and studious students being tasked with taking the lead on the content. The groupings give all students the opportunity to collaborate by teaching and learning from each other.

Estelle coordinated the Montebello Improvement Committee, which sought to more clearly illuminate the availability of helpful campus resources for students by identifying a staff member in each office willing to serve as a special helper. The committee also helped organize students to make and deliver small thank-you tokens to staff to express student acknowledgement and gratitude more clearly to staff. She led another collaborative effort, the Nursing Student Development and Retention Committee. The committee assembles well-respected staff, faculty, and administrators supportive of retention efforts to vet policies and activities. In both cases, the choice of collaboration followed the evidence base (shared responsibility for student success), reflected the institutional mission and strategic plan (student success), and reflected one of Estelle's strong interests.

The Power of a Positive Circle

Verlando Brown shares a powerful technique that always yields results and that even the most shy among us can learn to do.

Verlando Brown

Verlando Brown is just beginning his career in higher education. At 26, he has completed a master's degree in human services administration at the University of Baltimore. He is passionate about removing barriers to and opening opportunities for higher education for first-generation students. Although he is in the early stages of his career, he has already mastered a key strategy for being an effective and positive public servant. He consciously develops and nurtures a positive network of like-minded professionals and solicits their help on a coordinated and ambitious effort to empower first-generation students to reach their potential.

Verlando Brown's method relies on the characteristics shared by those drawn to public service: a strong work ethic, deep commitment, and resourcefulness. His tactics are simple but very time consuming. He makes networking a priority, and much of the time he spends on service is devoted intentionally to building, nurturing, and coordinating his network.

His first foray into networking occurred as an undergraduate. He sought assistance from faculty, academic advisors, and career counselors, asking them to recommend others who might have information and resources. Over time, these recommendations led him to higher levels of the university hierarchy. By the time he completed his undergraduate degree at Towson University, he was on a first-name basis with the president of the university.

Today, he builds his network in a wide range of settings. He has introduced himself to others in class, at work, or while volunteering. He always shares his passion for first-generation students, describing his overall interests in relation to his own story as a first-generation student. He freely shares his personal struggles about times when he did not know where to turn, and he describes how he discovered available resources by intentionally seeking help. Using the same strategy he used so effectively for his own success, he ends each conversation by asking for help with the cause of first-generation students. He asks each person to identify people from their own network who are interested in first-generation students. As did his initial personal attempts to seek help, his efforts help to build a network that includes people in decision-making positions. His network includes several university presidents, high-level school district officials, executive directors of local nonprofits, and foundation program officers. He nurtures this network through frequent and sustained individual contact. He keeps each member apprised of his progress and identifies new members of the network. As are the initial introductions, this aspect of networking is very time consuming.

The efficacy of his strategy is plainly visible through his coordination efforts. In 2015, he launched First Generation Baltimore. The aim of this initiative is to convene higher education leaders and first-generation students to foster additional institutional commitments to first-generation students, greater coordination among institutions, and utilization of available resources by first-generation students. He contacted 24 members of his network—representing universities, the school district, nonprofits, and foundations—to serve as the planning team; all agreed to serve on the team. At the first meeting, he did not need to convince anyone to contribute; he had already achieved that through his networking. Instead, each offered an immediate and tangible contribution during the first meeting. The foundations are donating space, food, and parking. The school district pledges data. Nonprofits are managing the online registration, designing the event, and inviting selected attendees. Coordination and collaboration of this breadth and scope is unprecedented in Baltimore. Verlando Brown achieved it on his first try: the power of a positive circle.

Strategies for Managing Difficult People

One of the most challenging, if not the most challenging aspects of higher education, is learning to work effectively with people we find difficult. Next we learn from a master in doing just that.

Lynne Damon

Lynne Damon's professional experience includes serving as a pro-posal developer, writer and federal grant administrator for several higher education institutions. Over the past twenty-five years, her positions included three inherent challenges. First, she had no formal line-authority over the staff tasked with implementing the grants. Second, grant-funded projects don't always include all of the staff tasked with implementation in the planning process which poses a risk for full staff buy-in during implementation. Third, as grant administrator she was responsible with ensuring that all project goals were met or exceeded. Lacking the authority to supervise the actions of others yet accountable for their outcomes, Lynne's track record show grant targets consistently met or exceeded.

Her secret? Learning how to manage difficult people of course.

Damon notes that "difficult" people come in many varieties.

At times, it may seem as if difficult people are *purposely* trying to make your life miserable. You may think they are consciously undermining your efforts to accomplish the task or work effort.

Regardless of whether any of this is true, when you have to work with difficult people, the challenge is to put aside your irritation and work together (when you have to). Damon suggests the following steps for dealing with difficult people.

Step 1

Put aside your irritation or anger and determine what needs to be accomplished.

Step 2

Open your ears and your mind.

I've found that no matter how difficult someone is, if you open your mind and listen carefully, there is usually new and/or important information to learn that will help your understanding of the task, situation or requirements.

Further, by listening carefully to what someone is saying, you can gain a better understanding of a person's needs, priorities, biases, objectives and key drivers.

Step 3

Focus on making each encounter positive and if possible, productive – ideally, with manageable goals and objectives. Sometimes these may be very small. Do not dismiss the seemingly insignificant because it is not the entirety of what you want or need to accomplish. Phone conversations and meetings each present unique opportunities. By seeing each encounter individually, it makes it easier to stay in the present, focus on the task or conversation at hand, and manage the situation and yourself as productively as possible.

Step 4

Remain clear about what you need to accomplish. It is very easy to become drawn into the drama of difficult people, by remaining clear about your objectives, it will help you through the twists and turns of the routes sometimes necessary to take when working with challenging people and personalities.

By staying clear on your overarching objectives, (while still remaining patient and controlling your irritation), you will be more able to find alternative routes and opportunities that you might otherwise have dismissed or overlooked due to your own personal inner dialogue.

In the end, it isn't about managing other people at all. It is about managing yourself. By focusing on managing yourself, on what you can do rather than what others are preventing you from doing, you eliminate the difficulties posed by difficult people. These strategies will put yourself in the best possible position to be positive and productive even in circumstances that you find difficult.

Questions for Reflection

1. What are the advantages and disadvantages of collaborating with others?

2. To make the most of the collaboration, what guidelines should be incorporated prior to the collaboration?

3. Who do you perceive to be the key stakeholders in higher education that should be involved in collaborations?

4. How will you measure the effectiveness of the collaboration?

5. What types of collaborations can take place between higher education and K-12 school systems?

6. How will you deal with conflict during collaborations?

7. Are there differences in collaborations based on gender, age, ethnicity, or economic status?

8. During your last collaboration, what are three lessons that you learned?

9. How do you maintain a positive circle in your professional life?

10. Name the people and organizations in your network. What are some ways that you will grow and utilize your network?

My Higher Education Journal

Please use this space to respond and reflect on the ideas presented in this chapter for your own professional growth.

2

Maximizing Professional Development Opportunities

Introduction

A DRIVING FACTOR behind our decisions to enter public service in higher education is the opportunity to have a positive, meaningful, and lasting impact. Our ability to have a meaningful impact fuels our energy and optimism and keeps us in the field of higher education. We work hard to create the conditions that foster student success by developing innovative courses and honing teaching skills to facilitate student learning. We also draw more students into the discipline, guide students in preparation for graduate study or rewarding careers, and offer a wide array of other services. At the same time, we often engage in professional development opportunities or professional learning to enhance our skill set, better connect with our students, and contribute to the field. This chapter includes suggestions regarding formal professional development, finding resources to pay for furthering your education, and meeting and exceeding goals. Taken together, these strategies can help you maximize the connection between your efforts and your impact.

5 Tips for Professional Development

Professional development and professional learning engage us as lifelong learners in ongoing development to enhance the skills and abilities needed to do our work. Professional development opportunities usually involve a common interest for participants and range from face-to-face to multimedia activities. Below are several suggestions for making the most of professional development opportunities.

Tip 1: Find the Time for Professional Development

Although we often recognize the benefits of professional development, it is not always easy to find the time to pursue these activities. We are often bombarded with tasks and responsibilities at work—committees, projects, emails, or teaching responsibilities—with deadlines requiring immediate attention. If you cannot take the time to attend a conference, there are many other avenues for *professional development*, such as watching a webinar online, joining a discussion board, having lunch with a mentor, or creating a professional development opportunity at your company or college.[22]

> *"All that is valuable in human society depends upon the opportunity for development accorded the individual."* —Albert Einstein

---

22   http://www.myacpa.org/professional-development-opportunities

Tip 2: Grow Through Networking

Use the professional development opportunity as an avenue to grow through networking with others. Often we attend professional development opportunities related to our field, job, or an interest that we would like to explore. As you attend workshops, conferences, or meetings, you will meet people with similar interests, and you may want to stay connected. Plan in advance for networking and bring your business cards. Also, you can network online through LinkedIn, Twitter, blogs, and social media. These resources offer additional ideas[23] and a *rationale for networking.*[24]

"Networking is marketing. Marketing yourself, marketing your uniqueness, marketing what you stand for." —Christine Comaford-Lynch

Tip 3: Expand in Different Roles

Professional development opportunities include those obtained through experience. One way to expand in a different role is to step out of your comfort zone. For example, if you have a fear of presenting in front of others, doing a *presentation* on a topic that you enjoy can help you to overcome those fears and build your self-confidence.[25] You might also *expand your skill set* by organizing, planning, and leading a conference, workshop, or meeting.[26]

---

23 http://www.educause.edu/research-and-publications/books/tower-and-cloud/social-networking-higher-education

24 http://www.forbes.com/sites/glennllopis/2012/05/29/7-reasons-networking-can-be-a-professional-development-boot-camp/

25 www.skillsyouneed.com/presentation-skills.html

26 http://projectmanagementhacks.com/how-to-expand-your-job-the-pushing-boundaries-strategy/#sthash.7a0cYm6r.dpuf

"Fear stifles our thinking and actions. It creates indecisiveness that results in stagnation. I have known talented people who procrastinate indefinitely rather than risk failure. Lost opportunities cause erosion of confidence, and the downward spiral begins."—Charles Stanley

Tip 4: Cost-Effective Professional Development Opportunities

Although professional development funds through your college or university may not be available, other options are often overlooked: for example, scholarships or discounted conference registration in exchange for volunteering. Professional associations, companies, and colleges offer professional development opportunities at little or no cost. Grants sometimes include funding for professional development.[27] Research, a positive focus, and determination open up professional development opportunities.

"Successful people maintain a positive focus in life no matter what is going on around them. They stay focused on their past successes rather than their past failures, and on the next action steps they need to take to get them closer to the fulfillment of their goals rather than all the other distractions that life presents to them." —Jack Canfield

---

27   www2.ed.gov/about/offices/list/ope/news.html

Tip 5: Share with Others

Even if not required by your funder, share the experience and knowledge you gained with others. You can report at meetings, do a presentation at a retreat, or post a summary of the experience online, thereby allowing others to benefit from your professional development. Sharing your professional development activities not only helps others; it also refreshes the lessons you learned.[28]

"Nothing liberates your greatness like the desire to help, the desire to serve." —Marianne Williamson

5 Tips for Finding Resources for Graduate Study

Pursuing graduate degrees or coursework is another avenue for professional development. Without support, this is an expensive option; therefore, our tips focus on identifying funding sources. We are aware of the many benefits of attaining a college degree. Nevertheless, many people face challenges during their educational journey. One of the challenges that can be minimized is the stress of paying for college. When all else fails in finding money for college, most people obtain a student loan. Imagine, however, the freedom of graduating from college without owing a huge student loan. These are just a few tips on finding money for college. As part of your research, you should also inform other people about your plans to obtain a college degree and your desire to graduate from college with as little debt as possible. These people may know about financial resources as well. Above all, never let financing deter you from reaching your goal of attaining a college degree.

---

28 http://www.forbes.com/sites/work-in-progress/2013/07/25/5-ways-to-share-your-professional-expertise-and-4-reasons-you-should/

Tip 1: Do Your Research Before Enrolling

Locate websites by doing Internet searches, including Facebook.[29] Review the websites of the universities offering your desired field to learn about their institutional scholarships, grants, and fellowships. Books also serve as resources for graduate student support, for example Kelly-Tanabe's *1001 Ways to Pay for College: Strategies to Maximize Financial Aid, Scholarships and Grants*.

> *"By failing to prepare, you are preparing to fail."* —Benjamin Franklin

Tip 2: Bring Out Your Best on the Grant and Scholarship Application

Once you have identified universities that provide tuition funding, you need to focus on promoting yourself effectively on the admissions application. You can find help from several excellent websites.[30]

> *"Take advantage of every opportunity to practice your communication skills so that when important occasions arise, you will have the gift, the style, the sharpness, the clarity, and the emotions to affect other people."* —Jim Rohn

---

29 https://bigfuture.collegeboard.org/scholarship-search
30 http://www.gocollege.com/financial-aid/scholarships/apply/

Tip 3: Higher Education Commissions

Usually each state has a higher education or college commission overseeing state universities and providing financial resources (e.g., Maryland Higher Education Commission).[31] One of the advantages of scholarships and grants that are posted on the higher education commission websites is that they usually are not specified to a particular university. The grant or scholarship is generally targeted for a particular shortage area such as nursing. In addition, state legislators sometimes sponsor scholarships for students in their districts.

"My favorite words are possibilities, opportunities and curiosity. I think if you are curious, you create opportunities, and then if you open the doors, you create possibilities." —Mario Testino

Tip 4: Philanthropic and Professional Organizations

Many philanthropic and professional organizations provide scholarships. These organizations view scholarships as benefiting the student and the field as a whole. Search for organizations that represent your career field. Philanthropic Educational Organization (PEO) is one of many organizations that fund higher education opportunities.[32]

"Goodness is about character—integrity, honesty, kindness, generosity, moral courage, and the like. More than anything else, it is about how we treat other people." —Dennis Prager

---

31   http://www.mhec.state.md.us/FinancialAid/descriptions.asp
32   http://www.peointernational.org/

Tip 5: Seek Funding Through Any Means Possible

Be creative and search broadly for resources, including sources such as churches, banks, employer tuition reimbursement plans, businesses, and Go Fund Me pages.[33] Organizations providing small scholarships often have fewer applicants; assembling several such sources is a pathway to generate the total resources needed for tuition.

"By any means necessary." —Malcolm X

5 Tips to Maximize Your Impact by Meeting or Exceeding Goals

Lofty goals propelled our decisions to enter higher education. Seeing our impact relative to those goals requires that we translate abstract aspirations into concrete goals. The tips below offer a sequence of steps to do just that.

Tip 1: Start with Your Goal, Then Create Milestones To Reach It

Making progress toward those goals by setting intermediate milestones ensures that our impact will be regularly visible to us and will serve as a motivator.[34]

"Start with the end in mind." —Steven Covey

---

33   https://www.gofundme.com/
34   https://revathionline.wordpress.com/2011/07/22/time-management-breaking-down-tasks/

Tip 2: Take Regular Stock of Your Progress, and Refine, Redouble, or Redirect Your Efforts Accordingly

You are much more likely to reach your goals when you *assess your progress* at regular intervals.[35] Based on your progress, you can determine whether and to what degree your efforts are working and make midcourse corrections when necessary. Another effective strategy involves setting and monitoring SMARTER goals (Specific, Measurable, Achievable, Relevant, Timebound, Evaluated, Revised).

> *"Without reflection, we go blindly on our way, creating more unintended consequences, and failing to achieve anything useful."* —Margaret Wheatley

> *"The real man smiles in trouble, gathers strength from distress, and grows brave by reflection."* —Thomas Paine

Tip 3: Determine Whether Impact or Strategy Is Most Sacred to You

Our desire for impact is often accompanied by deep allegiance to our chosen process to achieve that impact. Only you can decide whether you are willing to abandon a beloved strategy if you discover it is not effective. But you must be honest with yourself about your potential for impact when you have chosen strategy over impact.

> *"I am of the opinion that my life belongs to the community, and as long as I live, it is my privilege to do for it whatever I can. I want to be thoroughly used up when I die, for the harder*

---

35   https://www.skillsyouneed.com/ps/reflective-practice.html

I work, the more I live. Life is no 'brief candle' to me. It is a sort of splendid torch which I have got hold of for a moment, and I want to make it burn as brightly as possible before handing it on to the future generations." — George Bernard Shaw

Tip 4: Identify Your Strengths and Use Them

Choosing the most effective strategies to achieve your goal is informed by assessing the skills, character strengths, and other resources you bring. For students, the concept of finding strategies that are most effective for themselves is called "productive persistence".[36] This same principle applies to us as higher education professionals.

"Success is achieved by developing our strengths, not by eliminating our weaknesses." —Marilyn vos Savant

Tip 5: Leverage Your Efforts by Conducting Them in a Group

Your efforts toward meeting your goals may be more effective when you collaborate and network with others. There are many benefits of building a collaboration and network to pursue your goals. Chapter 1 details steps on how to build an effective collaboration and network. In addition, collaboration relates to Habit 6, synergy, of Steven Covey's *Seven Habits of Highly Effective People* (Covey, 1989).[37]

"If you want to go fast go alone. If you want to go far go together." —African Proverb

---

36   https://www.carnegiefoundation.org/in-action/carnegie-math-pathways/productive-persistence/

37   https://blog.hubspot.com/sales/habits-of-highly-effective-people-summary

5 Tips for How to Make a Meaningful Career in Higher Education: You ask for it

For years, I have heard people (including myself) lament that their colleagues and supervisors "make" them do more than their fair share of time-consuming thankless tasks, that they do not recognize the obvious: how much we have already contributed to our institutions. The consequences are real: exhaustion, resentment, reduced time with family, compromised research agenda...and self-care tossed out the window. In truth, however, we are not compelled against our will. Instead, we pay this high cost for a distorted perception. The reality is that we can set boundaries and have much more control over what we will and will not do.... And they will still be pleased. An effective alternative is to follow a series of steps to an assertive response.[38] If you prefer, you can watch a video or read a document.[39] *MindTools* includes an excellent overview.[40]

Tip 1: Assess Yourself

The more precisely we are able to identify situations in which we are least assertive, the more effective our strategy to address those situations. Edmund Bourne's *Anxiety and Phobia Workbook* (2015) includes an assertiveness questionnaire to determine your level and areas of assertiveness. A free online assertiveness questionnaire is available:[41]

---

38 http://psychcentral.com/blog/archives/2010/02/25/building-assertiveness-in-4-steps/

39 https://www.youtube.com/watch?v=ubSL1tFmgDc&feature=youtu.be, http://www.mirecc.va.gov/cih-visn2/Documents/Patient_Education_Handouts/Assertive_Communication_Version_3.pdf

40 https://www.mindtools.com/pages/article/Assertiveness.htm

41 http://psychologytoday.tests.psychtests.com/take_test.php?idRegTest=3195

"The most fundamental aggression to ourselves, the most fundamental harm we can do to ourselves, is to remain ignorant by not having the courage and the respect to look at ourselves honestly and gently."
—Pema Chödrön

Tip 2: Think About What You Really Want

What is really bothering you about this situation? What one thing do you want to request? Do you want to say no to a task or role? You are much more likely to be heard and understood if you make a single request. You might think your need is patently obvious, that everyone can see that what you are being asked to do is totally unreasonable. But you will get further if you assume instead that others will not recognize your need unless you tell them.

"I've learned that people will forget what you said, people will forget what you did, but people will never forget how you made them feel." —Maya Angelou

Tip 3: Remind Yourself That You Have the Right To Request and the Right To Say No

People who are drawn to higher education are highly committed to their institutions, their students, their disciplines, and higher education overall. This commitment spurs us on to assume ever more tasks as we know that if they are not completed students (the department, the institution…) will suffer. And this conviction has merit; we have all seen efforts go by the wayside when the core faculty/staff stops working on it.

"Nobody can give you freedom. Nobody can give you equality or justice or anything. If you're a man, you take it."
—Malcolm X

Tip 4: Prepare and Rehearse Your Response for a Calm Delivery

The "I" statement is your friend. It will not bring you 100% to your goal each and every time, but it is much more effective than complaining to colleagues, silently burning with resentment, or breaking into exhausted tears at a department meeting. For upcoming interactions that are predictable, you can prepare a response and practice it so that your delivery is calm and free of emotion.

Step 1: State the problem situation in terms of its consequence to you.

I understand that the department budget is due tomorrow and that Jim is out sick; however, I told my son I would go to his volleyball game tonight. I want to honor my commitment to him.

Step 2: State your request.

Can we come up with an alternative plan for completing the budget?

Step 3: Repeat if necessary.

If people don't understand or forget your request, you will need to paraphrase and repeat it.

Additional strategies and scenarios with example assertive and nonassertive responses are included here.[42] As so many assertiveness challenges in higher education involve setting boundaries, we include additional links from *Psych Central*[44], *Live Happy*[45], *Mind Body Green*[46], and a video. [47]

> *"Until you learn how to confidently say NO to so many things, you shall always say YES to so many things. The real summary of a regretful life is a life that failed to balance YES and NO. Yes! A life that failed to recognize when to courageously say NO and when to confidently say YES!"* —Ernest Agyemang Yeboah

Tip 5: Become the Broken Record

Identify your number one request, then repeat it as needed to make your point. For example, "I cannot take on any more committee assignments at this time."

A conversation with your department chair might go like this:

Chair: "I would like to assign you to xxx tenure review."

You: "I cannot take on any more committee assignments at this time."

Chair: "I really need you there, I know you will do a thorough job and his tenure review will be contentious."

You: "I cannot take on any more committee assignments at this time."

Chair: "But Phil and Joyce are on sabbatical; we don't have good choices for this committee."

---

42   http://www.psychologicalselfhelp.org/Chapter13/chap13_19.html

You: "I cannot take on any more committee assignments at this time."

Chair: "If you won't do it, I will have to ask John and he is under tremendous pressure to finish his second book."

You: "I know this is very important, but I cannot take on any more committee assignments at this time."

Need more inspiration? See Broken record examples[43]

"I encourage people to remember that 'no' is a complete sentence." —Gavin de Becker

---

43   http://www.gp-training.net/training/leadership/assertiveness/broken.htm

Spotlights – Professionals Who Stay the Course

This section features professionals who have mastered the tips recommended in this book. We hope their stories and strategies inspire you.

The Power of Professional Development

Shirley T. Thomas

Shirley T. Thomas embodies the purpose of professional development, which is to grow in one's occupation through learning opportunities. She regularly seeks and attends professional development opportunities to keep abreast of the best practices, strategies, and research to excel in her role as an adult educator and advisor. In realizing the value of teamwork and collective growth to reach departmental and institutional goals, Ms. Thomas shares the knowledge that she gleans from attending professional development opportunities. Not only does Ms. Thomas attend professional development opportunities, but she has also organized, planned, and implemented such opportunities for other adult educators. Thus, Ms. Thomas provides a great perspective on professional development as an attendee, colleague, and organizer.

Ms. Thomas entered the field of higher education 20 years ago. For 2 years, she was a reading instructor at Morgan State University. She has since spent the balance of her career at Coppin State University, where her experience includes program coordination, program development, special events planning, teaching reading and Freshman Seminar, tutoring, and advising students. She has a passion for student learning and is committed to encouraging students of all ages in their intellectual and personal development. Ms. Thomas believes that her previous stints in the corporate and nonprofit worlds have contributed to her rich experience base.

Ms. Thomas has a Bachelor of Arts degree in Journalism from the University of Maryland, College Park, and two master's degrees from Towson University: an MEd in Reading Education and an MS in Professional Writing. She is currently pursuing a doctoral degree in English at Morgan State University. Ms. Thomas refers to herself as an "obsessive-compulsive reader" who also writes in her spare time.

A.Yvette Myrick (AYM): Why do you think professional development is important in general?

Shirley T. Thomas (STT): Professional development is important for employees to learn about the latest developments in their fields and to develop new skill sets. I think that professional development activities keep employees energized and motivated; it keeps them from getting stale.

AYM: Why do you think professional development is important in higher education?

STT: One reason professional development is particularly important for those of us who work in higher education is because technology has changed the face of higher education. For example, many of today's students are opting to take online classes instead of enrolling in courses that meet in the classroom. Professional development activities allow higher education personnel to learn the latest in learning technology and how to best use it to instruct students. Professional development activities for higher education personnel are also important because today's student no longer follows the traditional student model of the 18-year-old coming directly from high school. Higher education today embraces a more diverse student body. Professional development activities can allow faculty to discover the best practices for teaching a diverse student population. Hands-on workshops and open discussion forums allow participants to share ideas with each other and to take these ideas back to their higher education institutions.

AYM: Do you think it is valuable for others to do their own presentations (breakout session or participation in a panel discussion) at a conference?

STT: I actually think any kind of participation during professional conferences is productive. From helping to coordinate the programs to sharing ideas as a member of a panel, these activities are all an integral part of the networking process.

AYM: How do you share your experience from a professional development opportunity with others?

STT: I engage in conversations with my colleagues and share what I have learned. I encourage them to participate in the professional opportunity the next time it is made available.

AYM: If you have planned professional development opportunities for other people, what was the overall experience that you wanted for the participants?

STT: I remember bringing publishing representatives to my campus to meet with the reading instructors. The purpose of the meeting was to train the instructors on how to use the technology that came with the textbook. I wanted the instructors to come away with at least a basic understanding of what was being presented. I also made sure that we could call the contact person to get answers to any follow-up questions that we had.

AYM: In closing, as you mentioned, professional development opportunities can motivate and inspire employees to grow through learning the latest developments in their fields. Professional development is particularly important in higher education, where the outcomes are so vital to the global economy. You identified key areas that higher education needs to continuously address if it wants to remain competitive in the global economy: technology and the changing student population.

In addition to your insight about the importance of technology and the changing student population in higher education, it was enlightening when you pointed out the power of networking at professional development opportunities. Sometimes, the personal and professional connections made from networking at professional development opportunities, such as meetings, conferences, or workshops, can be just as significant as the presentation that a person may have attended. On the other side of attending a presentation is conducting and presenting the presentation. It was informative when you shared the importance of planning a professional development opportunity for others, which can be an excellent way to grow and develop additional skill sets in organization and leadership. Thank you for sharing your valuable insights on professional development through the lens of an attendee, a colleague, and an organizer.

Finding Money for Graduate Study

Ginny Allen

Virginia "Ginny" Allen was born and raised in Baltimore, Maryland. After her high school graduation, she attended Goucher College for 3 years. She left college to marry and raise a family. Later, Ginny returned to college and graduated with a degree in business from Towson State University. Ginny excelled in a career in banking that included many positions and bank mergers. After her retirement in 1996, she was invited into the Philanthropic Educational Organization (P.E.O.) by her "big" sister from Goucher College. As an active member in P.E.O., Ginny found it to be the perfect environment through which to encourage women to pursue their educational goals through its programs and support.

A.Yvette Myrick (AYM): Can you briefly tell me about P.E.O.?

Ginny Allen (GA): P.E.O. is an organization through which women celebrate the advancement of women: encouraging women through scholarships, grants, awards, and loans and motivating them to achieve their educational goals. We own Cottey College in Nevada, Missouri for young women to attend college in a nurturing environment.

*For additional information about P.E.O, please visit its website: www. peointernational.org

AYM: Can you tell me some of the ways that P.E.O. helps women to reach their higher education goals through its scholarships and loans?

GA: We in P.E.O. actively look for women who are in need of financial support and fit their needs with our offerings, supplying encouragement and ideas that will make it possible for them to achieve their educational goals. For example, we provide a woman who needs help with money for a babysitter, transportation, books, or tuition with a grant from the Program for Continuing Education (PCE). The grant can provide financial assistance, and that little bit takes off some of the pressure. Through the Scholar Award, one of the awardees received money to travel to procure samples needed for a study for her PhD thesis. Through the International Peace Scholarship (IPS), we provide enough money that a foreign student can concentrate on her studies instead of taking on a job to supplement her income while in the United States. The Educational Loan Fund (ELF) provides a low rate loan to fill in the gaps for money needed for 3-4 years of college or a master's degree. My granddaughters have received this assistance. The interest is currently 2% simple interest, and the loan has a term of 8 years for payback, beginning at graduation.

AYM: I am also impressed by the P.E.O. STAR scholarship for high school seniors enrolling in a postsecondary institution upon graduation.

*For more information about the P.E.O. scholarships, please visit the following Web link: www.peointernational.org/peo-projects-and-philanthropies

AYM: Why do you think that some people do not access some of the millions of dollars in money that is available for people who seek a college degree?

GA: I think that there is not enough education on the use of the Internet as there are many categories of loans. There are books listing all sorts of loans—with specific criteria that are not even examined by students or advisors. Communication! Also, counseling and mentors are very important. That is why we are always looking for prospective applicants! The personal touch is so important, and that is why I am so excited when we are able to reach out to women in transition at any age!

AYM: What suggestions do you have for women who may not be eligible for P.E.O. funding, or for women who may not have received P.E.O. funding, but still wish to pursue a college degree?

GA: I would offer to go to the library and search the Web with her, helping her to locate sources to contact—and suggest the candidate meet with a college counselor for further assistance. We had a young lady who was unable to find a second cosigner, and we made several suggestions about asking for (financial) backing.

AYM: Thank you, Ginny, for sharing the wonderful things that P.E.O. is doing to make a difference in women's lives through its financial assistance. I was impressed to learn the following information from the P.E.O. website:

More than 90,000 women have benefited from our organization's educational grants, loans, awards, special projects and stewardship of

Cottey College. To date, P.E.O. has awarded Educational Loan Fund dollars totaling more than $143.6 million, International Peace Scholarships are more than $29 million, Program for Continuing Education grants are more than $43 million, Scholar Awards are more than $16 million and P.E.O. STAR Scholarships are more than $2.6 million. In addition, 8,500 women have graduated from Cottey College.

Well, based on the number of women who have benefited from its funding, P.E.O. has made a positive difference in not only the women's lives, but also their families, communities, and the global economy. Thank you again for sharing your wealth of knowledge and enthusiasm for an organization that is providing such great educational opportunities.

Meeting or Exceeding Goals

Katrina Concholar

Katrina Concholar has spent her professional life working in TRIO programs. Federal TRIO programs, established a half century ago under the Higher Education Act, focus on access to and completion of degrees in higher education for low-income students, first-generation students, and students with disabilities. TRIO is unique in the degree to which grantees are required to meet or exceed ambitious goals for college preparation, retention, graduation, and graduate admission. Over two decades, Katrina has hit her target every time. In her most recent TRIO position as director of a Talent Search program, Katrina increased the number of participants from fewer than 200 to more than 800 in a single year. And she achieved this while meeting the percentage targets, including the objective that 80% of its high school graduates would enroll in college. Needless to say, we are casting a spotlight on Katrina Concholar and discovering how she uses several of our five tips to consistently exceed her ambitious goals.

Katrina starts with the end in mind and then creates milestones to reach it.

Katrina breaks her annual targets into interim targets. These interim targets determine the timing of the recruitment events, school visits and student contacts, and program activities. In turn, the schedule of events determines the nature and timing of the behind-the-scenes work necessary to conduct these events.

Katrina takes regular stock of her progress and refines, redoubles, or redirects her efforts accordingly.

Bringing programs from good to great is Katrina's specialty. Using the milestones, she meets with her team weekly to measure progress against those milestones and identify the midcourse corrections needed to meet future milestones. This approach of regular review and revision is data-driven decision making at its best.

Katrina identifies her strengths and uses them.

Katrina relies heavily on her organizational talents and charisma to get the job done. She makes lists, uses whiteboards for timelines, and sets clear expectations and guidelines for her staff. She also recognizes that students, parents, and colleagues are drawn to her dynamic personality and positive energy. She uses this strength to recruit new students, motivate staff, and lobby for institutional resources. In each successive position, she hones these strengths, adding to her mastery of them and their potential to help her reach her goals.

Assertive Communication

Betty Webster

Betty Webster (BSN, MSN) developed her assertive communication skills throughout her career. Working in a variety of settings—from floor nurse to nurse supervisor to program director—she honed her skills working with patients, students, colleagues, supervisors, and subordinates. She is highly regarded for her conflict management skills and is often sought by colleagues to help develop assertive responses. Betty currently serves as director of the Catonsville Nursing Program at the Community College of Baltimore County (CCBC).

I can think of no better person than Betty Webster to spotlight for assertive communication. Her advice follows:

Overall, you want to be aware of your trigger points with a person. Once you have clarity on that, you can move toward a rational plan for assertive communication.

When you have a conflict, you can diffuse tension by responding with "my perception of what you said/did is...." Instead of coming off as a direct accusation and putting the other person on the offensive, using the term *perception* invites the person to reply with an alternative explanation that corrects or elaborates your initial statement.

Take the exchange as an opportunity to listen intently to understand and acknowledge their point of view. Don't interrupt but let them talk until they are completely finished. The simple act of being listened to without interruption is rare and effectively addresses many frustrations. When you respond, spend time asking questions so you clearly understand their perspective.

When you have a conversation and are not prepared to respond to a question or request, always remember you can ask for time to think it over. "I need time to think about that and I will get back to you."

If you are predicting an interaction, prepare for it by clarifying the goal. What is your purpose for this interaction? Once the goal is clear in your mind, the best strategies to reach that goal will be easier to identify. Having a clear goal also helps you have self-restraint during a conversation as you understand that making impulsive statements will make you stray from your goal.

At first this can be hard, but your efforts to forge even a small sincere personal connection ("How did your grandson enjoy his baseball game on Saturday?") can yield significant dividends. Pay attention to personal topics that make the person light up and ask about those. The goal is not to push yourself too hard, but rather to identify small areas of sincere connection to build trust, appreciation, empathy, and likability.

The following are other Betty go-to phrases:

- I am confused. Is your concern X or Y?

- I really appreciate the fact that...

- Can you please give me your rationale behind that decision?

- I'd like to take a pause for a moment and back up to [previous point in conversation]...

- What you just said made me feel X, was that your intent?

- If you would like to tell me something, please tell me directly.

Questions for Reflection

1. What three professional development opportunities would you like to attend in the next year?

2. Name at least one professional development activity that you would like to lead or co-lead in the next year, such as a presentation at a conference. What are your goals and desired outcomes for the professional development activity or presentation?

3. What do you think is the difference between assertive and aggressive communication? Which communication style do you think represents you? Why do you identify with that communication style?

4. What two milestones would you like to accomplish in reaching your 1-year and 5-years goals?

5. Do you think that gender or ethnicity plays a role in whether or not a person asks for what they want professionally and whether a person is comfortable with saying "no" to a request?

6. What things can you or your institution do to lessen the cost for participation in the professional development opportunity?

7. What are three professional development organizations that focus on your field or discipline?

8. Do you think that there should be leadership training in higher education based on gender? Why or why not?

9. How do you share your knowledge with others?

10. What can you do or have you done for professional development on the international level?

My Higher Education Journal

Please use this space to respond and reflect on the ideas presented in this chapter for your own professional growth.

3

Enhancing the Student Experience

Introduction

FOSTERING STUDENT ENGAGEMENT—The time and effort students devote to educationally purposeful activities—is an educator's central task (Hu & Kuh, 2001). As higher education professionals, we have a wealth of knowledge related to our subject matter and beyond. Yet, being knowledgeable in a subject matter does not necessarily equate to being knowledgeable about engaging students in the classroom. To be effective facilitators of learning, we need mastery of our subject matter as well as mastery in engaging our students in the learning environment. This chapter looks at two sets of strategies educators can use to make their classes more meaningful, interactive, and engaging. The first involves direct faculty-to-student interactions, and the second involves integrating technology. In addition, this chapter includes a special resource developed to promote engagement and self-reflection called GIFTS: Goals, Intelligence, Family, Transition, and Self-Efficacy.

5 TIPS FOR Engaging Students in the Classroom

Tip 1: Create a Welcoming Environment for Learning

The first thing that a student notices when he or she walks into the classroom is the actual classroom learning environment—before looking at the syllabus or getting to know you. Therefore, the physical classroom space should be bright, comfortable, and inviting for students. The placement of the desk, laptop, and projector should facilitate the students' being able to see each other and the instructor without any obstacles blocking their view. The instructor should be enthusiastic and eager in each class session. This type of environment makes students want to engage.

"Our environment, the world in which we live and work, is a mirror of our attitudes and expectations." —Earl Nightingale

Tip 2: To Build Engagement, Instructors Should Recognize That Each Student Is an Individual

Class size makes individual treatment a challenge, but meeting this challenge is critical. Strive to develop an individual success plan for each student. Some students may need assistance with writing or citing sources. Other students may need support in the areas of time management and balancing class responsibilities with other life commitments.

"Think twice before you speak, because your words and influence will plant the seed of either success or failure in the mind of another." —Napoleon Hill

Tip 3: Focus on Student Participation and Discussions

In large-class lecture environments, student voices can become silent, thereby inhibiting active and engaged student learning. Create opportunities for every student to speak, for example, by breaking classes down into small discussion teams.

"A new word is like a fresh seed sown on the ground of the discussion." —Ludwig Wittgenstein

Tip 4: Provide Timely and Constructive Feedback with Positive Reinforcement

Students rely on timely and constructive feedback to understand how to improve in preparation for the next assignment. Instructors should provide supportive and encouraging remarks to each student despite the student's performance on the assignment. For example, if a student did not perform well on a test or writing assignment, the instructor can say, "Good effort...we will work together to continue your path to success in the class."

"Everyone has inside of him a piece of good news. The good news is that you don't know how great you can be! How much you can love! What you can accomplish! And what your potential is!" —Anne Frank

Tip 5: Take Into Account Different Learning Styles

Some students are visual, others more auditory, while some prefer hands-on or kinesthetic styles of learning. Thus, instructors must vary their instruction techniques to engage all students.

"Education in our times must try to find whatever there is in students that might yearn for completion, and to reconstruct the learning that would enable them autonomously to seek that completion." —Allan Bloom

5 Tips for Integrating Technology and Pedagogy

Introduction

Advances in technology not only impact our personal and work lives but they also have a major impact in education. Technological advances in education are demonstrated in various forms, such as the format of teaching students through distance education, enhancing and incorporating technology in the curriculum. Michael Fullan (2013) and our spotlight Valerie Riggs are the sources of the five tips on educational technology. Dr. Fullan is a Professor Emeritus at the Ontario Institute for Studies in Education at the University of Toronto. He has expertise in accomplishing whole-system reform in provinces, states, and countries. He has written numerous award-winning books that have been published in many languages.

Tip 1: Irresistibly Engaging

As Fullan (2013) elaborated, "...it [time management] means to be rapt, or in a state of 'flow' where time has no meaning" (p. 33).

"Time management is an oxymoron. Time is beyond our control, and the clock keeps ticking regardless of how we lead our lives. Priority management is the answer to maximizing the time we have." —John C. Maxwell

Tip 2. Elegantly Efficient

Fullan (2013) explained that the new products can be challenging, but they should also be "simple to get hooked on and natural to use...so the learning can be easier and more interesting" (p. 33).

> *"Success is no accident. It is hard work, perseverance, learning, studying, sacrifice and most of all, love of what you are doing or learning to do."* –Pele

Tip 3. Technologically Ubiquitous

In a global society, technology must be able to be globally available. As Fullan (2013) pointed out, technology should be "at our disposable 24/7" (p. 34).

> *"Technology made large populations possible; large populations now make technology indispensable."* —Joseph Krutch

Tip 4: Steeped in Real-Life Problem Solving

The curriculum should have problem-solving projects to facilitate "learning that creates the conditions for individual and group success on a global scale" (Fullan, 2013, p. 34).

> *"When it is obvious that the goals cannot be reached, don't adjust the goals, adjust the action steps."* —Confucius

Tip 5. The Instructor Does Not Have To Be a Technology Expert

The spotlight for education technology, Valerie Riggs, offered a tip. She noted that teachers do not have to know everything about technology. Teachers can include technology little by little, and the classroom community can work collaboratively to explore content with the technology to achieve their goals.

"The secret of concentration is the secret of self-discovery. You reach inside yourself to discover your personal resources, and what it takes to match them to the challenge." —Arnold Palmer

Spotlights – Professionals Who Stay the Course

This section features professionals who have mastered the tips recommended in this book. We hope their stories and strategies inspire you.

Engaging Students in the Classroom

Dr. Nelda Nix-McCray

We feature Dr. Nelda Nix-McCray as our spotlight for engaging students; not only is she a mastery educator, but she also excels in facilitating student engagement. Dr. Nix-McCray uses a variety of innovative strategies, such as music, pop cultural influences, and sociological theory to engage the learner and to enhance the learning environment. Dr. Nix-McCray has made a successful career by thriving in higher education. She is a coordinator of anthropology and sociology and associate professor of sociology at the Community College of Baltimore County, in Baltimore, Maryland. Dr. Nix-McCray has been a higher education leader for more than 20 years. She has focused on developing courses in the traditional classroom as well as hybrid and online environments that provide active engagement for student success. As an administrator, Dr. Nix-McCray mentors incoming department faculty and provides leadership and training in the classroom. In addition, she works to ensure that all courses are meeting department and college expectations regarding student outcomes. The tips from this chapter come directly from Dr. Nix-McCray's 25 years of experience in the classroom. She notes, however, that as the student population changes, educators must also change and evolve in their profession to meet students' needs.

Dr. Nix-McCray credits her early influences as an educator to her parents and great K-12 teachers. In particular, she credits the amazing college professors at the historically Black college and university (HBCU) she attended, who encouraged her when she was a student. Dr. Nix-McCray said that she originally wanted to study biology and has an undergraduate minor in biology. Her professors at the HBCU told her that she could be anything she wanted to be, however, such as a doctor of psychology or a doctor of sociology. After she started taking some sociology courses, she found her passion in sociology. She said, "Everyone [at the HBCU] made me and my classmates feel that we could do anything that we wanted to do." Indeed, she successfully progressed as a student in higher education and earned a bachelor's degree in sociology, a master's degree in sociology, and a doctorate in higher education. Dr. Nix-McCray is married and has two daughters in high school.

Dr. Nix-McCray offers suggestions to help faculty learn student names, a key strategy to show that you see each student as an individual. A full-time instructor can teach four classes a semester with 100 new students each semester. Use the opportunity to put a face with a name early on by returning weekly assessments or quizzes. During the first week of class, have the students say their first names when they speak; this helps you and the other students learn each other's names.

On many college campuses, the classrooms are evolving technologically to keep up with students' different learning styles. Dr. Nix-Cray encourages instructors to take full advantage of technology such as the smart classroom: "Make the most of the smart classroom to incorporate YouTube, music, whiteboard, and put ideas on a map," she said. She also allows some students to use their laptops and smartphones as a resource for classroom learning.

Dr. Nix-Cray believes that one of the great things about college classrooms today is that they are very diverse. Thus, it is not uncommon to have students from multiple generations, racial, cultural and socioeconomic backgrounds and lifestyles. She said, "You can have one class where there is a student who is 60 years old, retired, and just coming to take a class for personal enrichment [paired] with a student who is 18 years old as a discussion partner. So, it opens up a variety of different topics from multiple points of views and experiences." This level of diversity creates the perfect environment to share rich stories and varied perspectives in class discussions.

These tips are only a few in Dr. Nix McCray's treasure chest for student engagement. From her personal educational journey as a college student to the culmination of 25 years of teaching adult learners, she knows what it takes to be an engaged student. From setting the tone of a welcoming environment the first day of class to seeing the students as individuals, fostering student participation and discussion, providing timely and constructive feedback, and taking into account students' learning styles, student engagement is a continuous process. As her college professors engaged her as a student, Dr. Nix McCray is paying it forward by utilizing her position as a college professor to engage her students.

The Importance of Educational Technology in Higher Education

Valerie Riggs

Ms. Riggs embodies an educator who fully embraces and advocates for the importance of educational technology to enhance the field of higher education. She is an innovative educator, with more than 10 years of teaching experience at all levels of higher education. Furthermore, she continuously strives to keep abreast of the best practices in educational technology to incorporate in her classes. Ms. Riggs also plans to make a significant contribution to the field through her research in instructional technology while working on her Doctor of Education degree. Additionally, Ms. Riggs eagerly shares her skills and knowledge with others by presenting at professional development sessions. Thus, Ms. Riggs provides a great perspective as an educator, doctoral student, and researcher regarding the importance of educational technology in higher education.

Valerie Riggs is a faculty member in the Teacher Education and Professional Development department at Morgan State University. She has a BA in Sociology from University of Maryland, College Park, an MEd from University of Maryland, Baltimore County with a concentration in Urban Education and Instruction, and an MEd from Towson University with a concentration in Instructional Technology. She is currently pursuing doctoral candidacy in the Urban Education Leadership EdD program at Morgan State University. Her research interests are curriculum development and online course design.

Valerie is passionate about working with underprepared students and helping them to persist. Her research interests are focused on determining best practices for working with underprepared students in distance learning environments. She is also passionate about preparing students for 21st-century teaching by using the latest instructional technology tools. Ms. Riggs enjoys her family, friends, two dogs, traveling, running, and vacationing at the beach.

A. Yvette Myrick (AYM): How do you think that technology has impacted higher education?

Valerie Riggs (VR): Technology is at the forefront of many colleges and universities; however, technology changes every day and there are still many institutions of higher education that struggle to keep up with the changes. Technology and access to technology are the dividing barriers between global societies. Currently, in higher education there is a tremendous shift to incorporate technology physically and socially. In addition to understanding course content, students are also responsible for understanding how to use and apply technology resources to that content.

Course formats are also evolving and many new forms of learning are being implemented. In addition to traditional, hybrid, and online courses, there are now many open courses, such as MOOCs (massive open online courses). A MOOC is an online course that is open to everyone. It can be on any subject and the enrollment is unlimited. Students can get a small taste of what they could learn or they can complete a full series in an open format with many others. The varying forms allow for small numbers [of students] in the classroom or even up to thousands.

Institutional structure is also changing as a result of technology. In addition to traditional brick and mortar institutions, now there are virtual colleges and cloud-based organizations. Technology has changed the way students, faculty, staff, and administrators view and participate in higher education.

AYM: Why do you think it is important to incorporate technology into the curriculum?

VR: I think that it is extremely important to incorporate technology into the curriculum as well as our own pedagogical practices as educators. Today's students are 100% different from the students that we taught 20 years ago, 10 years ago, or even 5 years ago. Millennial students are multitaskers. They prefer to collaborate, research, explore and discover...sometimes all at the same time. What better way to meet their needs than to provide access to multiple forms of technology and media while they are learning? We need knowledge of technology to remain competitive in this ever-changing world. Technology in the classroom and incorporated into the curriculum provide the global link to resources that are necessary for millennial students to explore academic content and make real-world meaning for themselves.

AYM: Do you have any suggestions for how to incorporate technology into the curriculum?

VR: I follow the work of Michael Fullan. His latest text, *Stratosphere* (2013), discusses many ways that educators can implement technology within their curriculum and classroom. One key idea that Fullan referenced is the importance of incorporating "stealthy interventions". These interventions involve combining the social aspects, psychological aspects, content, and technology within the curriculum. The intervention can be a small-group assignment that requires the use of technology to solve a real-world, content-related problem. The interventions should be small and inexpensive; they should offer ease of technology use to avoid creating added stress for the student or teacher. Also, I think that it is important for teachers to believe that they do not have to know everything about technology. Teachers can create a small inclusion of technology, little by little, and the classroom community can work collaboratively to explore content with the technology to achieve their goals.

AYM: Thank you so much for sharing your insight on the importance of educational technology in higher education. You made some excellent points about educational technology. As you mentioned, one significant benefit of educational technology is that it can bring higher education to both individuals and masses of people and can be delivered in various formats. Unfortunately, for those global societies that do not have access to educational technology, it can also be a dividing barrier.

If we, as educators, do not incorporate educational technology into the curriculum, we will not meet the needs of our students, especially the millennial students. If we do not fully meet the needs of our students, we will not prepare students to compete in a global economy. Sometimes, educators are somewhat apprehensive about incorporating technology in the curriculum because it is new to them, and they may fear how they will look in front of their students if the lesson incorporating technology does not go as planned. But, as you pointed out, educators do not need to know everything about technology. You provided sage advice about incorporating something small in the curriculum as a means of getting started. Thank you again for sharing your valuable insight on the importance of educational technology in higher education.

Resources

GIFTS: Goals, Intelligence, Family, Transition, and Self-Efficacy

As higher education faculty, we are often faced with a diverse population of students journeying together on the same short path to successfully complete our class and move a step closer to achieving their long-term educational goals. An engagement activity that can create an avenue through which a diverse group of students can discuss, reflect, and write about the key components in their educational journeys is called GIFTS: Goals, Intelligence, Family, Transition, and Self-Efficacy. GIFTS is a socio-psychological intervention activity that covers several major topics related to students' thoughts about themselves and college. Socio-psychological intervention has been described as "brief exercises that do not teach academic content but instead target students' thoughts, feelings, and beliefs in and about school" (Yeager & Walton, 2011, p. 268). Socio-psychological interventions target students' achievement, not only in a particular class, but also for months and years after the class has ended.

There are certain criteria of socio-psychological intervention that can make it more effective: The activity should be implemented by an instructor who values the students and believes in their potential to persist and excel in college, the activity should not stigmatize, and it should not be introduced as one designed to help them feel positive about themselves (Yeager & Walton, 2011). For example, it should be introduced as a way to help a high school student who is contemplating attending college but struggling to complete high school. Because it is a college class, such an activity is an excellent opportunity to share videos and/or reading assignments and to have group discussions on key GIFTS topics, such as Carol Dweck's self-theories of intelligence (2000), effective goal development, and Bandura's theory of self-efficacy (1977; 1982). The activity should be brief and completed within the first few weeks of the course. Afterwards, students should not be required to share the outcome of their activity, but there could be a class discussion so that students could reflect on anything they would like to share about the process of completing the activity.

The activity would be implemented after reading assignments, viewing videos, or participating in group discussion. See links below for additional information:

Carol Dweck's self-theories of intelligence are presented in a TED Talk, *The Power of Believing That You Can Improve*[44] and another video *Two Mindsets of Intelligence*[45]. More on goal development is included in *Writing S.M.A.R.T. Goals.*[46] Self-efficacy is described in *Self-Efficacy: Helping Students Believe in Themselves.*[47]

---

44 http://www.ted.com/talks/carol_dweck_the_power_of_believing_that_you_can_improve
45 http://www.megsonline.net/lee_meg3.pdf
46 http://www.hr.virginia.edu/uploads/documents/media/Writing_SMART_Goals.pdf
47 http://serc.carleton.edu/NAGTWorkshops/affective/efficacy.html

GIFTS: Goals, Intelligence, Family, Transition, and Self-Efficacy

My Educational Journey

Your help is needed to motivate a student who is struggling with his or her studies in high school but is still interested in attending college. You can help in sharing your educational journey by writing a letter of support and encouragement to the high school student. Before you write your letter, reflect on your educational journey by responding to the topics below in GIFTS: A Self-Reflection. In your letter to the student, mention your GIFTS. Thank you for sharing the GIFTS from your educational journey with a future college student.

GIFTS: A Self-Reflection

Goals: My long-term goal that will be completed in 5 years is:

_____

My short-term goal, connected to my long-term goal, completed within six months to one year is:

_____

Intelligence: I have a growth mindset about intelligence because I:

_____

Family: The family members (and/or friends) who motivate and encourage me are:

_____

Transition: I made the transition to college at this point in my life because:

_____

Self-efficacy: I know that I will persist and graduate from college because I will do the following things:

_____

Sample socio-psychological intervention activity created by A. Yvette Myrick

Questions for Reflection

1. What are some ways through which you engage your students that were not covered in this chapter?

2. How do you know if engagement activities are effective?

3. Do you think that the methods needed to engage students are the same or different from 10 years ago? Which methods are the same? Which methods are different?

4. In what ways do colleges or adult education programs engage their students?

5. What role, if any, do technology, global economy, employment, community, family, relationships, and financial aid play in student engagement?

6. What are the advantages and disadvantages of utilizing technology in higher education?

7. In what ways have you incorporated technology in your curriculum? Are there other ways in which you would like to incorporate technology in your curriculum?

8. In what ways has technology impacted higher education other than in the classroom?

9. Do you think there is digital divide with students in higher education? If so, how should this be addressed, and who are the stakeholders needed to address this problem?

10. What educational technological advance do you think is needed to better serve students and adult educators?

My Higher Education Journal

Please use this space to respond and reflect on the ideas presented in this chapter for your own professional growth.

4

Service and Diversity

Introduction

THE NEED FOR a strong connection between higher education and the community is undeniable. The community needs higher education institutions to provide the skills, education, and talent needed to flourish on both the local and global levels. Central to the institutional mission of most universities is service to a diverse community. The connection should be one of interaction and reflection to make sure that both the community and higher education are growing and prospering together. Thus, the dilemma is not whether or not there is a strong connection between higher education and the community but how to effectively build this strong connection. In this chapter, we present five tips to connect higher education to the community to build an ongoing exchange of resources that produce positive outcomes in the community served. We also provide tips for building a diverse workplace central to academic excellence and equity.

5 Tips for Connecting Higher Education to the Community

Institutional missions move colleges and universities to facilitate social mobility. It is vital that both higher education and the community maintain a connection and seek new ways to connect and partner for each to grow and prosper.

Tip 1: Maintain the 3 CCCs (Communication, Connection, and Collaboration)

Higher education must strive to maintain the 3 CCCs (communication, connection, and collaboration) in its partnerships with businesses, community resources, K-12 school districts, workforce centers, and other entities.[48] A strong partnership between higher education and the local workforce centers is a great opportunity to utilize the three CCCs to meet the needs of the college, students, and workforce and to grow the local and global economy at the same time.

> *"This world of ours...must avoid becoming a community of dreadful fear and hate, and be, instead, a proud confederation of mutual trust and respect."* —Dwight D. Eisenhower

Tip 2: Fiscal Responsibility Is Key

Higher education[49] should be fiscally responsible[50] so it can offer sustainable employment opportunities to people in the community.

---

48   http://www.governing.com/gov-institute/voices/col-linking-data-higher-education-workforce-development.html

49   https://studentaid.ed.gov/sa/about/data-center/school/composite-scores

50   http://www.ihep.org/sites/default/files/uploads/docs/pubs/the_need_for_institutional_fiscal_responsibility_final_february_2011.pdf

"Productivity is never an accident. It is always the result of a commitment to excellence, intelligent planning, and focused effort." —Paul J. Meyer

Tip 3: Promote the Arts

Higher education can promote culture and arts in the community.[51] The promotion and support of culture and arts provide a great avenue for showcasing the talents of the people in the community and students, staff, and faculty at the college.

"We write for the same reason that we walk, talk, climb mountains or swim the oceans—because we can. We have some impulse within us that makes us want to explain ourselves to other human beings. That's why we paint, that's why we dare to love someone —because we have the impulse to explain who we are." —Maya Angelou

Tip 4: Provide Resources

Higher education can connect to the community by providing scholarships and other financial resources to assist students in pursuing their educational and personal goals.[52]

"There are amazingly wonderful people in all walks of life; some familiar to us and others not. Stretch yourself and really get to know people. People are in many ways one of our greatest treasures." —Bryant H. McGill

---

51   https://www.planning.org/research/arts/briefingpapers/overview.htm
52   https://www.data.gov/education

Tip 5: Provide Quality Education

Higher education can connect to the community by providing quality, inclusive, and diverse educational programs of study.[53] The programs of study should cover an array of delivery options to fit the needs of the adult learners, such as traditional, online, or hybrid options.

> *"A good teacher can inspire hope, ignite the imagination, and instill a love of learning."* —Brad Henry

5 Tips to Fostering a Diverse Workplace in Higher Education

Although there are numerous benefits to having a diverse workplace, it is sometimes not actively pursued, or if pursued, it is not a priority at some higher education institutions. Higher education institutions should reflect the diverse populations they serve. The tips below provide strategies to build a diverse workplace in which students, staff, faculty, and the community can grow and prosper.

Tip 1: Prioritize Diversity

Start at the top and make diversity a priority as part of the vision and mission of the workplace.[54]

> *"An individual has not started living until he can rise above the narrow confines of his individualistic concerns to the broader concerns of all humanity."* —Martin Luther King, Jr.

---

53   https://www.usnews.com/best-colleges
54   https://edis.ifas.ufl.edu/hr022

Tip 2: Recruit, Recruit, Recruit

Recruit through job fairs, journals, and media that target minority populations.[55]

> *"Diversity: The art of thinking independently together."* —
> Malcolm Forbes

Tip 3: Allocate Resources Toward Effective Diversity Initiatives

Set aside funding or seek funding to recruit, train, maintain, and assess the effectiveness of diversity initiatives.[56]

> *"It is time for parents to teach young people early on that in diversity there is beauty and there is strength."* —Maya Angelou

Tip 4: Spread the Word – Diversity Is Good for Business[57]

Actively get involved in community and international outreach to bring awareness of the college and its career opportunities.

> *"We need to help students and parents cherish and preserve the ethnic and cultural diversity that nourishes and we need to help students and parents cherish and preserve the ethnic and cultural diversity that nourishes and strengthens this community—and this nation."* —Cesar Chavez

---

55 https://hub.jhu.edu/2015/11/30/faculty-diversity-initiative
56 http://www.gwblawfirm.com/wp-content/uploads/2013/12/5-Strategies-for-Promoting-Diversity-in-the-Workplace-11-19-13.pdf
57 https://www.extension.harvard.edu/inside-extension/why-inclusive-hiring-good-business

Tip 5: Become a Culture That Embraces Diversity

Create a culture in which all employees feel respected, valued, and appreciated so that potential employees want to work at the college, and once employed, are retained.[58]

> *"Ultimately, America's answer to the intolerant man is diversity."* —Robert Kennedy

---

58 https://www.researchgate.net/publication/44018738_Strategies_to_ Achieve_a_Diverse_Faculty_and_Staff

Spotlights – Professionals Who Stay the Course

This section features professionals who have mastered the tips recommended in this book. We hope their stories and strategies inspire you.

Building a Strong Connection Between Higher Education and the Community

Jill A. Ziemann

The connection between higher education and the community is stronger when there are people on both sides who work tirelessly to build collaboration and resources so that each side can thrive. Jill A. Ziemann is exemplary in building collaborations between higher education and the community in her role as Director of Go2Work Programs and Gateway/Women in Transition/GarCo Enterprise at Colorado Mountain College. Her programs provide needed resources to people in the community so that they can reach their personal, professional, and educational goals. Jill shared a wealth of knowledge derived from her years of experience in working in higher education and being an active player in and keeping the pulse of the community to provide quality services to the clients in her programs.

A.Yvette Myrick (AYM): Please tell me a little about your background of working in higher education and the community.

Jill Ziemann (JZ): I began my professional journey as a graduate assistant for Dr. Caryl Smith, the Vice Chancellor of Student Affairs at the University of Kansas. Dr. Smith was very involved in advancing women. Dr. Smith was also actively involved in my master's degree thesis entitled *Women in Kansas Higher Education Administration*. Presently, I have been working at Colorado Mountain College for the past 10 years as Director of the Go2Work Programs, which include Wo/Men in Transition (for parents seeking to return to college); Gateway (for parents on Temporary Assistance for Needy Families or TANF); Free Go2Workshops and Computer Job Skills Workshops; and finally, GARCO Enterprise, a management training program in collaboration with the Department of Human Services. These programs' sustainability depends on partnerships with the community, especially the Board of County Commissioners, Human Services Commission, and the local Workforce Centers. I am also actively involved with many non-profits such as our local domestic violence shelter; Catholic Charities, Salvation Army; our local food banks and thrift shops; and Alpine Legal Services. Finally, through the years, I have developed relationships with businesses, foundations, and private individuals to support students in emergencies and provide essential needs (transportation, childcare, and housing).

AYM: What problems and opportunities do you think are impacting the community?

JZ: Students in these programs are not ready for work or education if they do not have what I like to call the "trifecta of success"—housing, childcare, and transportation. [For students] living in the rural resort area of Colorado, all three of these necessities are expensive and create barriers to completing their education and stabilizing their families. Student parents have to work and take classes; if they cannot make rent or they need snow tires to get their children and themselves to school safely, they are less likely to complete their courses successfully. I am alarmed at the times when something as small as needing windshield wipers can impact students' learning. In communities that are as caring as ours, finding the resources to quickly support students is as easy as knowing the right person to ask and setting up communication pipelines.

AYM: What role do you think higher education should play in the community?

JZ: Collaboration. Through the Go2Work Programs, we have been able to identify the greatest barriers and work together, not duplicating services. It is important for community colleges to have staff visible on committees that are addressing local concerns. We recently hosted Rural Philanthropy Days, which bring funders from urban areas out to rural communities to identify local needs and meet those organizations and nonprofits that need access to revenue. Colorado Mountain College plays a huge role in addressing the needs of our local workforce, local employers, and our large immigrant population. Our local schools are soon to consist of primarily minority students, and our college's vision, mission, and strategic plan reflect the importance of diversity in supporting the economic vitality and quality of our community.

AYM: Are there any ways to build a stronger connection between higher education and the community?

JZ: Back in 2008 when the economy fell, our Workforce Region Director asked the college if we could expand the Gateway program to every displaced worker. Gateway had been offering for parents on TANF classes on campus that focused on job coaching/life coaching/basic computer skills. We were able to obtain a grant and developed free, drop-in Go2Workshops for anyone in our community to get help with résumés, interviews, job searches, and online job applications. We found these to be instrumental in recruiting students for ESL, high school equivalency (HSE), and traditional as well as technical programs at Colorado Mountain College. Workforce staff attend and conduct scheduled assessments. We encourage all participants to register with their local workforce online in the workshops. That way, they can access information about careers and financial aid programs provided through the Workforce Innovations and Opportunity Act (WIOA). We soon learned that computer literacy was one of the greatest barriers to increased income, job advancement, and education. Through a series of grants, we now offer free computer job skills workshops that are very popular with this target population and also with local seniors who are interested in learning more about social media. The workshop curriculum is modular based and offers the basics from MS Office to WordPress. Finally, we have a semester meeting via IVS (interactive video system) with workforce and relevant CMC staff discussing concerns, new programs, and plans.

AYM: Is there anything that you would like to add about the connection between higher education and the community that we did not address?

JZ: Most important, our communities are small towns with small town values. When we reach out to help a student, whether it is just a simple act of kindness or assistance, it reflects out to the entire community.

Several years ago, our college began a "No Barriers" fund through our Foundation. Any student may apply for a small amount of assistance for an emergency or short-term need. The local campus (we have campuses in seven communities) has a committee that quickly supports this student, allowing us the opportunity to help directly rather than stressing other local nonprofits' resources. This also gives us the opportunity to identify students who might benefit from follow-up and encouragement along their educational and career pathway. These students often pay back or forward the support by becoming more involved in campus activities and their classwork.

I am always impressed when staff and instructors involved on the "giving" side of helping a struggling student benefit as much as the student! The sense of building relationships and meeting community needs leads to higher morale and value of their own role as educators and support staff.

AYM: Thank you so much, Jill, for sharing your input on how higher education can connect to the community. Your hands-on experience in connecting higher education to the community through programs and grants is beneficial in understanding the impact that each resource has on the others. Through your programs, you are able to listen and interact with the people in the community who often are most in need of the services and resources provided by higher education. You do an excellent job of keeping a pulse on the needs of the community and knowing how to effectively and efficiently address those needs. In other words, you are like the "community whisperer" to the clients and community that you serve. Based on the wealth of knowledge that you shared, it is evident that the community thrives when it is connected to higher education. Similarly, higher education cannot thrive unless it plays an active role in the community. There is a strong connection between higher education and the community, but it should not be taken for granted; it must be continuously evaluated, nurtured, and developed.

Fostering a Diverse Workplace in Higher Education

Lizbeth Jacobs

Lizbeth Jacobs was born in Guatemala City, Guatemala and moved to San Antonio, Texas at the age of 12. Lizbeth has not only lived a life impacted by diversity, but she also works diligently to foster diversity in education. Prior to graduation from high school, Lizbeth was accepted to West Point; however, despite her living in the state and her mother's paying taxes, the residency that she received the month after graduating from high school was not granted in time to change her status from student-visa to U.S. permanent resident for financial aid. Because of her status, Lizbeth would have had to pay out-of-state tuition ($25,000 per year plus a one-way open-ended ticket to her home country); therefore, she elected to enroll in a community college—still paying out-of-state rates. She graduated with a BA in English from the University of Maryland–University College in Heidelberg,

Germany and studied in England, Ireland, France, Spain, and Italy. She is enrolled at the Harvard Extension School to pursue a master's degree in English.

Professionally, Lizbeth has been involved in outreach work and community education for as long as she can remember. As a very young girl of 11, she taught adults the alphabet and helped her family conduct advocacy and community development in impoverished areas of Guatemala City. She has continued with this passion for outreach work and community development. This passion is evident in her lectures on American culture, immigration, and integration in countries such as Germany and Japan. Additionally, she teaches English as a second language to all age groups and serves as an adjunct faculty member at a college in Colorado where she teaches various subjects in English and Spanish.

Lizbeth and her husband Michael, now retired, have lived in many cities in the United States and abroad. Along with their adopted cat Nina (beloved puppy Shima recently passed away), the couple, married for almost 20 years, consider themselves extremely fortunate to call Colorado home since 2014. In her free time, you will likely find Lizbeth binge-watching TV with Nina and Michael, exploring Colorado's beauty, or on a plane heading for an expedition. She is deeply inspired by her marathoner sister and is often persuaded to run a 5K, 10K, or the very occasional marathon.

Lizbeth is passionate in her belief that everyone should have access to a great education. She stated, "It is my belief that education is not just a ladder up, but that it also opens doors, builds bridges, and develops understanding among different cultures." Through her life journey as a world traveler and adventurer, Lizbeth knows the power that a community can have on an individual. She also knows that education has allowed her to see the world and create rich and lasting relationships and asserts that it can be a tool to achieve the most unlikely of outcomes. Lizbeth has a diverse background, professionally and personally, and promotes a diverse workforce in higher education.

As the diversity of the student population continues to increase, there should also be an increase in the diversity of faculty, staff, and administrators who work in higher education. As Lizbeth pointed out, diversity in the people who pursue careers in higher education is important because we are often a product of our environment. Lizbeth provided a relevant example: She described spending 3 weeks in Texas to help her sister move. Prior to going to Texas, she had been advised by her doctor to become gluten-free. She did try, but was unsuccessful. She said that it was not until she visited her sister in Texas and saw her sister eat gluten-free, that she was able to apply that habit to her life. As a visual learner, Lizbeth believes that a key factor was that she "saw" how it was done and now has been gluten-free for 3 months and plans to continue to remain gluten-free. Similarly, when others see minorities work in higher education careers, they may think that they can also have a career in higher education.

Lizbeth pointed out that the lack of diversity in people who are in higher education careers often "leads to stereotypes that become perpetuating myths, but also self-fulfilling prophecies." To elaborate, Lizbeth pointed out that intelligence is not the only conclusion to explain the many Indian (heritage) doctors. She posed the question, "Is it possible that more and more children become doctors because they have someone in their family and at large in their community whom they have seen follow a career in medicine?" Likewise, being in an environment through family or the community can inspire others to strive for a career in higher education.

In the pursuit to be successful in any career, one may face obstacles along the way; however, there may be additional obstacles faced by minorities in pursuing higher education careers. One obstacle that minorities may face is navigating the educational system early during the educational journey. Lizbeth described a time early in her educational journey when she encountered obstacles as a minority and foreigner. She noted that she did not receive "college counseling" in high school because her school counselor assumed that she was not going to college. Also in high school, Lizbeth said, "in spite of an almost perfect grade point average, the fact that I was a foreigner prevented me from getting into English honors classes." Further, her sister, who was reading Tolstoy, Gabriel Garcia-Marquez, and Pablo Neruda by the time she was 10 was still held back a year in high school because she was coming from another country. While in high school, Lizbeth's mother encouraged her to go to college, but as an immigrant, her mother did not know how to help her daughter accomplish the goal at that time.

Unfortunately, as Lizbeth pointed out, some parents have long work schedules to support their families and some have language and cultural barriers. Then, as was the case for Lizbeth, the children must learn to advocate and navigate the educational system themselves. These obstacles early in the educational journey can derail some people from ultimately attaining a college degree, which is often needed for a career in higher education.

Another obstacle that minorities face is that they are often categorized as being "behind" in some areas in education. There is often a lack of understanding about why this situation persists. In the category of minorities, Lizbeth includes homeless teens that face their own set of obstacles. Lizbeth shared that minorities could be "anyone who doesn't benefit at large from the same educational and economic system that the rest of the population [does]." In college, Lizbeth said that she was behind and had to catch up in her studies. With many people the constant battle of being behind and catching up can create obstacles that may seem insurmountable at times. Nevertheless, seeing other people overcome obstacles like these can be a true motivator.

Another obstacle is the cost of higher education. For many people, minorities in particular, paying for higher education without the benefit of scholarships or grants can place a financial burden on individuals and families that can be difficult to overcome. Lizbeth faced this obstacle while pursuing her goal of attaining a college degree. Because her academic records were not accessible at the time to apply for scholarships, she resorted to student loans. Later, after she had access to her records, she applied for and received scholarship funding for her college education.

For most people, the ideal economic situation would be to remain debt free. Therefore, after graduating with a bachelor's degree, some people postpone attaining a graduate degree because they want to start their careers and start earning money, fearing that even less funding is available for students pursuing a master's or doctoral degree. Also, some people are not encouraged by family members to pursue a college degree or a high-paying professional career. Lizbeth faced these dilemmas as well as the struggle of coming from an immigrant family for which survival was the priority. Although it may have taken a little longer than she anticipated for enrollment in graduate school, she is excited because she said, "I am 40 and only now figuring out how I am going to graduate school at Harvard Extension." Unfortunately for others, the obstacles of not being able to navigate the educational system, being behind in school, and not being able to afford the cost of a higher education degree can make it challenging to pursue a career in higher education.

Higher education institutions can play a major role in increasing diversity in their workforce. A significant way that higher education institutions can increase diversity in their workforce is through community and global outreach. "Outreach work is arduous, but I believe one of the only ways higher education institutions can change the culture," Lizbeth said. Higher institutions can do outreach by actively recruiting students who are graduates or about to graduate by attending job fairs sponsored by historically Black colleges and universities (HBCUs) or Hispanic serving institutions (HSIs). They can also notify the career counselors at these institutions of their job openings. Through these connections and outreach between the higher education institutions and HBCUs and HSIs, a network can be formed that promotes a mutual goal of diversity in higher education careers.

Another way that higher education institutions can increase diversity in their workforce is to make it a priority in their vision and mission; however, diversity in the workforce must go beyond just being part of a written statement. There must be a concerted effort to make the goal a reality. An example of a higher education institution's demonstrating that diversity in the workplace is a priority is Johns Hopkins University (JHU). In 2015, Johns Hopkins launched its Faculty Diversity Initiative to support expansive and inclusive faculty searches, create a pipeline of diverse scholars, and broaden support for underrepresented members of the faculty. They also committed more than $25 million in new funding to the faculty diversity efforts over the next 5 years. Many higher education institutions may not have the funding of JHU to create a diversity initiative of this magnitude, but they can develop other initiatives programs that demonstrate that diversity in the workforce is a priority.

Embracing diversity in the workforce is not only vital for the higher education institutions and their employees, but it also has a positive impact on the student population. As Lizbeth said, "a diverse work force eliminates the false stereotype bias." She pointed out that when people see others that look like them in careers such as the Indian doctors, President Obama, or presidential candidate Hillary Clinton, it can inspire them to be anything that they want to be. Similarly, in higher education, when students see diversity in the workforce such as a minority who is an academic advisor, professor, or president of the college, it becomes a teachable moment about the possibility of a career in higher education.

Questions for Reflection

1. What are the economic, educational, and residential needs of your community?

2. In what ways does your institution connect to the community?

3. In what ways can your institution build its connection to the community? What resources and staff are needed to build this connection?

4. Where do you see the community 5 years from now? What role does the institution play in this vision?

5. How does your institution build the connection to the international community?

6. In what ways do you define a diverse workplace, such as race, ethnicity, age, socioeconomic levels, or something else?

7. Using a rating of Excellent, Fair, or Poor, where does your institution rate for diversity in the workplace? Why did you give your institution the rating?

8. What suggestions can you make for creating a diverse workplace? Which people and resources are needed?

9. Does your institution have a vision and mission statement that mentions diversity and/or culture? Are the workplace actions, policies, environment, administration, staff, and/or faculty aligned to the vision and mission statement? Why or why not?

10. How can you and your institution work with the community to foster diversity in the workplace?

My Higher Education Journal

Please use this space to respond and reflect on the ideas presented in this chapter for your own professional growth.

5

Research Focus

Introduction

HIGHER EDUCATION FORMERLY involved two clear professional tracks: a research-focused position at a research (R1) university or a teaching-focused position. Increasingly, publication requirements at teaching universities are central to tenure decisions. It is no longer an option to focus on excellence in teaching and advising; we must all learn the art of publication. This chapter approaches this topic from two angles. The first presents 5 tips for building a viable research agenda and spotlights a person who has done just that. The second introduces a specific strategy: incorporating evidence-based practices to improve student retention. This strategy creates the raw material for ultimately publishing the results of your work in the classroom, as an advisor, or in another role affecting student retention. Either way, it is time to bring out your inner researcher.

5 Tips for Advancing Your Research Agenda

Tip 1: Protect Your Research Time

The tenure clock demands publications. The time you can devote to research competes with fixed required commitments (e.g., teaching schedules, meetings), nonroutine requests (e.g., tenure reviews, letters of reference), and your own desire to improve your teaching and service activities. The immediacy of these competing priorities requires you to impose an effective barrier around your research time to ensure that you continue to make progress. To create this barrier, take stock of your day's rhythms. What times during the day involve the fewest interruptions? Are you able to log off your email and turn off your phone during your research time? See the Pomodoro technique Tip #3 in Chapter 7 Self- Care for one strategy to manage interruptions of your research time. See also the meeting and exceeding goals section in Chapter 2 Professional Development for tips on establishing priorities. There are other strategies for protecting your research time.[59]

"It is not enough to be busy; so are the ants. The question is: What are we busy about?" —Henry David Thoreau

"The best time to plant a tree was 20 years ago. The next best time is today." —Chinese proverb

---

59 http://www.raulpacheco.org/2014/05/protecting-your-time-as-an-early-career-academic/

Tip 2: Engage Daily in Research

There are several payoffs for including an hour of research in your daily schedule rather than reserving it to a single day.[60] First, by conducting research daily, you are putting your research into long-term memory; therefore, you do not have to start over each week to remember where you left off. Second, research is data collection, writing, *and* reflection. Your daily engagement is an opportunity to reflect. Third, this habit presents the opportunity for your research to be at the top of your mind, ready to reflect on as you read the news, stand in line, or go to work, adding even more engagement in research to your day.

"Do one thing every day that scares you." —Eleanor Roosevelt

"Don't count the days, make the days count."
—Muhammad Ali

Tip 3: Seek a Senior Faculty Coauthor and Mentor

Some universities have structured processes to match senior faculty to incoming junior faculty to provide guidance and coaching and, in some cases, to coauthor publications. This is such an effective strategy to learn the academic research ropes and gain publications that it is worth pursuing on your own if your institution does not offer it.[61] Among the many benefits are two core advantages: Senior faculty can (a) illuminate the institution's tenure requirements, making them more explicit; and (b) demystify and accelerate the publication process. See the section on networking in Chapter 2 *Maximizing Professional Development Opportunities* for strategies to connect with potential senior faculty mentors and coauthors.

---

60 http://www.ascd.org/publications/books/107006/chapters/Memory,_Learning,_and_Test-Taking_Success.aspx
61 http://graduate.iupui.edu/doc/faculty-staff/mentoring-lit-2.pdf

"There is nothing I like better than conversing with aged men. For I regard them as travelers who have gone a journey which I too may have to go, and of whom I ought to inquire whether the way is smooth and easy or rugged and difficult. Is life harder toward the end, or what report do you give it?" —Plato

Tip 4: Do Not Let the Perfect Be the Enemy of the Good

Academics hold very high standards for their work. Academic writing is also intensely personal; the finished page represents for all readers one's intellectual capacity. The instinct to keep revising endlessly until it is perfect is one outcome. Avoiding informal reviews by our peers is another. We can also feel a sense of paralysis and writer's block preventing us from even starting. Anne Lamott provides guidance in *Bird by Bird* on how to counteract these tendencies.[62]

"Books are never finished, they are merely abandoned." — Oscar Wilde

"We are all apprentices in a craft where no one ever becomes a master." —Ernest Hemingway

"Better a diamond with a flaw than a pebble without." —Confucius

---

62 http://www.profkrg.com/10-writing-truths-author-anne-lamott

Tip 5: Challenge Those Negative Thoughts That Stifle Your Research

Gaining control of your own self-defeating thoughts is vital to the creative process. Cognitive restructuring and meditation are two evidence-based strategies to do that. See also Chapter 7 Self-Care for step-by-step guidance on both strategies.

"The self-criticism of a tired mind is suicide." —Charles Horton Cooley

5 Tips for Using Research to Improve Retention Outcomes

Just over a decade ago, the National Survey of Student Engagement (NSSE) Research Institute set out to identify the common core of practices among high-performing institutions.[63] The Project DEEP (Documenting Effective Educational Practices) study included 20 institutions that had higher graduation rates than would be predicted given the entering characteristics of their student bodies.[64] The institutions represented the full range of higher education and included doctoral extensive, doctoral intensive, master's granting, liberal arts, and baccalaureate general institutions. The 20 case studies generated six mutually reinforcing institution-level principles for student success. These principles have stood the test of time. Although the principles are institutional in nature, individuals can enhance their impact by engaging in practices consistent with these principles.[65] These tips feature five of the six DEEP Conditions for Educational Success.

---

63   http://nsse.indiana.edu/html/projectDEEP.cfm
64   http://nsse.indiana.edu/pdf/conference_presentations/2005/naspa_2005_deep.pdf
65   http://nsse.indiana.edu/institute/documents/briefs/DEEP%20Practice%20Brief%206%20What%20Faculty%20Members%20Can%20Do.pdf

Tip 1: Practice Consistent with a "Living" Mission and "Lived" Educational Philosophy

Universities with a "lived" mission are more effective at engaging students.[66] A lived mission implies not only that a school's mission is easily articulated and resonates with students, staff, faculty, and administration, but also that it is used to guide and prioritize programs, policies, and budgetary allocations (Kuh, Kinzie, Schuh, & Whitt, 2005)[67].

> "A small body of determined spirits fired by an unquenchable faith in their mission can alter the course of history."
> —Mahatma Gandhi

Tip 2: Maintain an Unshakable Focus on Student Learning

DEEP schools share a belief that all students can learn and therefore preach and practice a "talent development" philosophy.[68]

> "I never teach my pupils. I only attempt to provide the conditions in which they can learn." —Albert Einstein

---

66 http://citeseerx.ist.psu.edu/viewdoc/download?doi=10.1.1.407.8730&rep=rep1&type=pdf

67 Kezar, A., & Kinzie, J. (2006). Examining the ways institutions create student engagement: The role of mission. *Journal of College Student Development, 47*(2), 149-172.

68 http://files.eric.ed.gov/fulltext/ED506529.pdf

Tip 3: Shared Responsibility for Educational Quality and Student Success

"What is common among high-performing schools is that a mix of administrators, faculty and staff members, and students work together to set direction and to create and maintain student success efforts" (Kinzie & Kuh 2004[69], p. 5).

> "It takes a whole village to raise a child." —Igbo and Yoruba Proverb

Tip 4: Clear Pathways to Student Success

High-performing institutions support students in meeting high expectations through clear and explicit performance standards, frequent and prompt formal and informal feedback, and scaffolding to support students every step of the way.[70] The Resources section of this chapter includes a handout of research-based study strategies guiding the cycle from reading, to class note taking, to exam study.

> "Train up a child in the way he should go: and when he is old, he will not depart from it."—Proverbs 22:6

---

69   http://nsse.indiana.edu/institute/documents/Kinzie%20&%20Kuh%20article.pdf
70   http://sc.edu/fye/events/presentation/sit/2005/pdf/C-51.pdf

Tip 5: Improvement-Oriented Ethos

Project DEEP institutions systematically incorporated assessment into their activities with an eye toward improving academic and student service delivery. These schools tended to underestimate their own performance. Several guides provide specific guidelines including the Minnesota Department of Health PDSA (Plan, Do, Study, Act) cycle, the *Mathetimatica Policy Research Report: A Conceptual Framework for Data-Driven Decision Making*, and the UNICEF guide: *How to design and manage equity-focused evaluations.*[71] [72] [73]

"What gets measured gets managed." —Peter Drucker

71   http://www.health.state.mn.us/divs/opi/qi/toolbopdsa.html

72   http://www.mathematica-mpr.com/~/media/publications/PDFs/education/
     framework_data-driven_decision_making.pdf

73   https://evalpartners.or/sites/default/files/EWP5_Equity_focused_evaluations.pdf

Resources:

Overview of Effective Study Strategies[74]

Overall Approach

Study Time Is Study Time

Eliminate distractions. Never multitask. Do not schedule other activities during study time. Include a 10-minute break during every hour of study. During the break, rest your brain by doing a relaxing activity such as taking a walk or folding laundry. Never stimulate your brain or distract yourself with, for example, your phone or Facebook. Study at the same time in the same place to harness your brain clock. It takes you 40 minutes to shift from one topic of concentration to another. But when you study at the same time and the same place, it takes only 10 minutes!

Your Brain Is Your Best Friend—Work with It!

The strategies below work with all learning styles. When you work with your brain, you learn faster, remember more, and understand at a deeper level. Never forget that your brain is a muscle – it needs rest, healthy food, and exercise to work at top capacity.

Keep Your Eyes on the Prize

Start and end your day by remembering why you are doing this. Keeping your goal at the forefront is the best strategy to tackle procrastination and distractions.

---

74 Adapted from Robinson, F. R. (1970). *Effective study* (4th ed.) New York: Harper & Row.

Before Class—Read

Question – narrow your focus to scan for relevant information.
Read over your learning objectives.

- Turn each learning objective into one or more questions. Your reading will be directed to answering these questions.

  » Do your best here; don't worry if your question is not perfect.

- Reflection questions: Spend a few seconds asking yourself:

  » What do you already know about this topic?

  » How is it related to topics you already know?

Survey – global overview of chapter contents, provides purpose to your reading.

- Prioritize your reading. Begin with the most important reading.

- Read the title, boldface headings/subheadings, introduction and summary, charts, diagrams, and chapter review questions.

- Identify headings related to your learning objectives and note page numbers.

- Notice reading aids: italics, boldface print, charts or other visuals. Read – read with a purpose, quickly scanning the text to answer the questions.

- Look at the relevant charts/diagrams and scan the identified sections to identify the answers to your learning objective questions. Once located, stop to skim paragraph(s).

- Write your summarized/chunked and paraphrased notes from the readings. Chunking, or summarizing in seven words or less, is efficient because it forces you to process the information before taking notes *and* the brain absorbs information seven bits at a time.

- Important: Put the page numbers, textbook name, and learning objective number on the notes.

During Class—Record

Record – during the lecture take strategic notes on the PowerPoint.

- Reread learning objectives and reading notes immediately before class.

- Date and number note pages.

  » Using the learning objectives to focus your attention, write notes to elaborate any new points made by the professor.

  » Important: Put a star next to any point that is repeated or indicated by the instructor as important.

  » Listen first until you understand the instructor's point before writing your notes.

  » Use abbreviations; paraphrase and chunk your lecture notes.

After Class—Do Something with the Material

Do Something with the Material

- Multimode makes memories. You remember 20% of what you read, but 90% of what you read, hear, see, say *and* do.

- Participate in a study group.

- Reflect on the material you just learned.

  » Reread your lecture and reading notes the same day as the class because the information is fresh.

  » Cover up your reading and class notes and recite 24, 48, and 96 hours later to commit it to long-term memory.

  » Look for connections between the text, notes, and any hands-on practice. Compare to previous week's material. How can this material be applied? What new questions are raised? What is more confusing? What is clearer?

- Create a study guide for the most critical or confusing information.

  » Reorganize and condense your lecture and reading notes into a study guide answering the learning objectives.

  » Make a chart, concept map, or outline to reorganize and summarize the key points.

  » Recite your study guide 24, 48, and 96 hours later to put it in long-term memory.

  » Combine several learning objectives into a single study guide

- Practice test questions.

- Once a week, take a practice exam.

- Strategy: Cover the response categories before reading the question. Visualize the answer. Then find the answer in the response categories.

- Read and understand the rationales for correct and incorrect answers.

- Analyze the results: Use the feedback provided to identify areas for study.

Preparing for the Exam

- By keeping up along the way using effective strategies, you have already done 95% of your studying for the exam.

- 4-5 days before the exam, make a detailed study plan. Prioritize topics according to your areas of weakness and budget your available study time accordingly.

- Compartmentalize the topics. Study one topic at a time. Review the PowerPoint and study guides. Do practice test questions. Based on the incorrect answers and answers you got right only because you guessed, go back and review the details of that topic. Test yourself again to confirm your mastery.

- Be realistic. Take into account all of your obligations outside school and hold yourself accountable.

Spotlights – Professionals Who Stay the Course

This section features professionals who have mastered the tips recommended in this book. We hope their stories and strategies inspire you.

Advancing Your Research Agenda

Janet Davis

Janet Davis is an associate professor at the University of Texas at Austin. Since 1998, she has published two books and 15 peer-reviewed articles or book chapters. A third book is due out this spring. She also has a strong teaching record, with five teaching awards. Coupled with her research and teaching record, she also served as chair of her department and took on a number of major administrative projects serving her institution. She is very active as a public humanities scholar and has served as an advisor for ten museum exhibitions across the country and nine documentary films. She has been twice invited to write opinion pieces for the *New York Times*. She shares her take on our tips for research below.

Tip 1: Protect Your Research Time

Initially, Janet established Friday as her research day. Inevitably, however, meetings or other mandatory activities occurred on Fridays and ate away at her research time. She tried another strategy: to sign up to teach classes in the morning and then do her research in the afternoon. In this case, the office day did not end after her classes were over. Instead emails or conversations generated the need for follow-through that day. Again, her scheduled research time was eroded. Now she conducts her research in the morning before heading to campus. She has found a time of day when it is easiest to protect her time and which complements her productivity.

Tip 2: Engage Daily in Research

In addition to moving her research time to the morning, she shifted from a-day-a-week model to conducting her research an hour a day. She found that with the Friday-only schedule, she spent a good part of her day refamiliarizing herself with her project. With the daily routine, she is constantly connected to it and her research is always on her mind. It fosters incidental reflection, as thoughts and ideas about her research percolate in her mind or are informally exchanged with colleagues. In this way, the one hour really multiplies itself. An hour a day is sufficient to make progress, but if you do more…. Great!

Tip 3: Seek a Senior Faculty Coauthor and Mentor

Janet advises:

> If your institution has a junior faculty mentoring program, you should take advantage of it. Senior faculty possess a wealth of information regarding all aspects of life at a research institution, including the process of publishing your work, maintaining a productive balance between your research and teaching time, and giving you direct feedback on your scholarship. Research is not a solo enterprise, so take advantage of the opportunity for others to review and respond to your research. If your institution does not have a faculty mentoring program in place, you should forge these relationships with your colleagues, understanding that some faculty will be more amenable to mentoring than others.

Tip 4: Don't Let the Perfect Be the Enemy of the Good

Her view used to be "I am not publishing anything that is not great," but now she subscribes to the adage that all of your work is a work in progress. When doing the original archival research trip for her upcoming book, Janet applied this principle. Rather than continue to collect data until she thought she had a perfect amount, she set out to develop a manuscript from the material she had gathered during the trip. She did exactly that and the book is due out this spring.

She encourages junior faculty to take all opportunities to have others review and respond to their work. "Conference presentations are a great entry point to introduce your work and network. It will give you deadlines to force the public display of your good work to get the feedback needed to make it excellent work."

Tip 5: Challenge Those Negative Thoughts That Stifle Your Research

When conducting research, you have two voices vying for your attention: "You are great" or "You suck. You better give it up." Using meditation techniques and cognitive strategies is essential to determining which voice you will hear.

Other Tips

She used to think that the research process was linear, with two parts: First she did her research; then she wrote. But now she believes research is simultaneous to writing and those two are connected with much reflection.

In preparation to submit to a particular journal, she advises reading many articles in that journal to familiarize oneself thoroughly with the structural elements, format, and such. Look very carefully at the submission requirements, which will go a long way toward demystifying the journey to publication.

Using Research to Improve Retention Outcomes, and Sharing Responsibility for Student Success

Ayana Shannon-Johnson

Over the course of her career, Ayana Shannon-Johnson has served as a personal trainer, resident hall director, college access program specialist, and retention coordinator. The unifying theme to these positions is her focus on empowering people to reach their personal goals. And one of her most effective strategies to leverage her efforts is research based: sharing that responsibility with others.

As Ayana sees it, sharing responsibility for student success means that we are co-mentors for our students. Using our own words and drawing from our own bag of tricks, we reinforce each other's efforts to foster student motivation, engagement, initiative, and self-advocacy...and everything else that supports students in reaching their goals.

Her strategy for identifying ideal co-mentors is time tested and has worked in all of her positions. When she needs a co-mentor from a particular area, she starts with the staff directory and methodically calls each person until she identifies people who are spontaneously helpful. Those helpful people become part of her "shared responsibility co-mentor" circle. Immediately after the call, she writes a short but sincere thank you note with a specific acknowledgement. She nurtures the relationships by sharing information and professional development opportunities that will make their job easier and more meaningful.

For Ayana, sharing responsibility includes her students. During her initial conversations when meeting students, she asks them to identify their short- and long-term goals. Seeing her role as connecting them to where they want to go, she coaches them to identify the small steps leading to their goals. Now having articulated their goals and action steps, she can serve as their accountability partner[75] for regular check-ins, further planning and problem solving, and encouragement.

---

75   http://www.goal-setting-guide.com/the-role-of-an-accountability-partner-in-goal-achievement/

Questions for Reflection

1. What is your research agenda? Why did you select this research agenda?

2. What three things are you currently doing or will you do to advance your research agenda?

3. Some colleges and universities have a mandate of "publish or perish" as a means of promotion or job security. Do you agree or disagree with this mandate? Why or why not?

4. Name at least three publications, such as professional journals, to which you would like to submit an article for publication.

5. In what ways do you plan to make significant contributions to your professional field or academic discipline from your research?

6. Name three things that you think are important factors in student success.

7. What three strategies do you think impact student retention?

8. Do you share responsibility with others for student success? If so, who are the people or departments with which you share this responsibility?

9. How do you set up expectations with students that they also share a responsibility in their educational success?

10. How do you handle situations when people or departments are not upholding their part in student success?

My Higher Education Journal

Please use this space to respond and reflect on the ideas presented in this chapter for your own professional growth.

6

Careers in Higher Education

Introduction

CAREER PATHWAYS TO higher education are as varied as the individuals choosing higher education careers. This chapter provides tips for following a few of those pathways and highlights exemplary professionals forging those paths. They range from making a deliberate search with a career in higher education an explicit goal to pursuing careers outside the United States. We highlight people who pursued a self-taught pathway to their profession and those who moved from the K-12 system to higher education. We also include careers in health care that are linked to higher education.

5 Tips for Thriving in Leadership Roles

Leadership roles can be perceived as a calling or a curse. At times, for some people it can be seen as both. Some people are put in leadership roles, whereas others seek leadership roles. Whether you sought the leadership role or it was thrust upon you, embrace and excel in it for your duration in the position. Your professional reputation and self-confidence can be impacted by your performance in the leadership role. In the big picture, the leadership role can be just one piece of the puzzle in your professional profile or it could be several pieces that make up most of the puzzle. It is important to make the most of the time that you are in the leadership role.

These tips provide steps needed to help you excel in leadership roles in higher education or in another type of organization. Following are 5 tips for leaders to achieve success in their leadership roles.

Tip 1: Be Mission Driven

Develop a clear vision and mission to set a path that you want to follow.[76] You may develop this on your own or in collaboration with others. Without a vision and mission, it is difficult to lead others to achieve the change and results desired.

"Great leaders communicate a vision that captures the imagination and fires the hearts and minds of those around them."
—Joseph B. Wirthlin

Tip 2: Establish Short- and Long-Term Goals

Setting goals helps provide motivation and direction for action steps. See also Chapter 2, *Maximizing Professional Development Opportunities*, for tips for meeting and exceeding goals.[77]

"Setting goals is the first step in turning the invisible into the visible." —Tony Robbins

---

76 http://ctb.ku.edu/en/table-of-contents/structure/strategic-planning/vision-mission-statements/main
77 https://www.mindtools.com/pages/article/smart-goals.htm

Tip 3: Seek Feedback

As much as possible, elicit feedback and input from others, especially the people directly impacted by the decisions. Working as a team affords opportunities for people to contribute their skills, education, and experience.[78] Remember, communication is one of the greatest keys to success.

"I know of no single formula for success. But over the years I have observed that some attributes of leadership are universal and are often about finding ways of encouraging people to combine their efforts, their talents, their insights, their enthusiasm and their inspiration to work together." —Queen Elizabeth II

Tip 4: Keep Up with Your Profession

You should be aware of the latest advances in your field. The world is constantly changing and evolving. You and your team can keep abreast of changes and advances through professional journals, conferences, networking, and professional development opportunities. Through your leadership, you and your team may be the people who are making significant contributions and leading the advances in your field.

"The growth and development of people is the highest calling of leadership." —Harvey S. Firestone

---

78   http://www.effectivemeetings.com/teams/teamwork/effective.asp

Tip 5: Practice Self-Care

Take leadership of yourself by tending to your physical and mental state. It is difficult to lead others if you are not at your highest level both physically and mentally. Michelle Martin's blog *The Bamboo Project* is a rich source of strategies and perspectives for self-care for professionals.[79]

> *"Success in its highest and noblest form calls for peace of mind and enjoyment and happiness which come only to the man who has found the work that he likes best."* —Napoleon Hill

5 Tips for Job Search in Education

Careers in higher education include student services, teaching, operations, or administration. While working in higher education, a person can focus in one area during his or her entire career or move from one area to the next area. In addition to a variety of different careers in higher education, a person can work at a 2-year, 4-year, private or public, nonprofit or for-profit, HBCU, liberal arts, research college, or university. In other words, a variety of job opportunities and colleges can lead to a long, rewarding career.

Tip 1: Use Job Search Websites

There are job search websites through which you can create a specialized job search profile for yourself and select the criteria for salary range, geographic location, job title, and much more. You also can set up the job search so that the website can email you daily, weekly, or monthly alerts to keep you updated on the latest job announcements.

---

79   http://michelemartin.typepad.com/

Glass Door[80], Indeed[81], and Beyond[82] are general job websites. Websites specific to higher education include Higher Education Recruitment Consortium[83], Higher Ed Jobs[84], and Inside Higher Ed.[85]

"Success is almost totally dependent upon drive and persistence. The extra energy required to make another effort or try another approach is the secret of winning." —Denis Waitley

Tip 2: Work Part-Time Positions

Often, especially for teaching, full-time professors start in adjunct positions so they can establish themselves in an academic department. Colleges and universities advertise these positions on their websites.

"No matter how small and unimportant what we are doing may seem, if we do it well, it may soon become the step that will lead us to better things." —Channing Pollock

Tip 3: Network

If you are searching for a job in higher education, contact your college alumni association and career services department to see if they have professional connections to people who work at colleges and universities. In small regional areas where there may be only one or two colleges or universities, building position relationships through

---

80 www.glassdoor.com
81 https://www.indeed.com/
82 www.beyondjobs.com
83 https://www.hercjobs.org/index.html
84 https://www.higheredjobs.com/?locale=en_US
85 www.insidehighered.com

networking is one of the key factors in building your career. So, reach out to associates, friends, or family members who may already have connections or work at colleges or universities. Also, create or update your LinkedIn account with your career summary, educational background, and work experience to build your network and promote yourself.[86]

"When people rely on surface appearances and false racial stereotypes, rather than in-depth knowledge of others at the level of the heart, mind and spirit, their ability to assess and understand people accurately is compromised." — James A. Forbes

Tip 4: Relocate

Ideally for many people, it would be great to find a job that does not require a long commute from home or relocation; however, the ideal job for you in higher education may not be in your local area. You may need to consider jobs in other areas that may make it necessary to relocate to another part of the state, another state, or another country. The good thing is that the college or company may help with the relocation costs. Also, relocating for a job opportunity can enhance your skill set and résumé. Career One Stop provides additional information on relocating.[87]

"It is good to have an end to journey toward; but it is the journey that matters, in the end." —Ernest Hemingway

---

86   https://www.linkedin.com/
87   www.careeronestop.org

Tip 5: Professional Development

By attending conferences, webinars, professional development opportunities, and professional learning activities in higher education, you are accomplishing several things at one time. First, you are increasing your knowledge in the area of interest. Second, you are meeting and networking with other professionals who share similar interests. Third, you are learning about ways to showcase topics of interest to sharpen your presentation skills. The American College Personnel Association includes other professional development opportunities.[88]

5 Tips for Transitioning from a K-12 Career to a Higher Education Career

The transition from a secondary classroom to college teaching is not as difficult as one might expect. K-12 professionals bring with them training and experience of tremendous value to the college classroom. Their expertise in student classroom engagement, active and collaborative pedagogies, and learning outcome assessments are directly transferable to the college classroom. This situation stands in contrast with the case of faculty entering directly from graduate school, who must gain this type of expertise in the classroom.

Tip 1: Networking in Higher Education

Perhaps during your time working in a K-12 career you met some contact people through working together on projects or committees or through other avenues. You may also have family, friends, or former colleagues who are working in the higher education field. Reach out to your contacts and let them know that you are considering a career change into higher education. You can ask your contacts about

---

88   www.myacpa.org/professional-development-opportunities

their work experiences in higher education or something else as part of your research. Please see Chapter 1 Collaborating and Networking Are Necessary for additional tips on networking.

> *"You can wonder forever how many teeth a horse has—or you can find a horse, open its mouth and count its teeth."* — Barbara Sher

Tip 2: Join Higher Education Professional Organizations and Subscribe to a Higher Education Journal

By joining a higher education professional organization and subscribing to its journals (usually the journals are free or low cost for members), such as College Reading and Learning Association (CRLA), you can connect with people who share similar interests at the organization's annual meeting or conference.[89] Another great professional organization is the American Educational Research Association (AERA), because it covers research in K-12 as well as higher education.[90] By joining the professional organization and subscribing to the journals, you can learn about some current issues, themes, and prominent research in higher education.

> *It is a universal principle that you get more of what you think about, talk about, and feel strongly about."* —Jack Canfield

---

89   https://www.crla.net
90   www.aera.net

Tip 3: Do Volunteer Work in Higher Education

Consider being a volunteer at a college or university before making a major career move to determine if it is something that you really want to pursue.[91] Working with adults is very different from working with children. Adults have their own characteristics and face real-life challenges such as working full-time jobs, raising children, dealing with adult relationships, and other issues, while at the same time attending college. It is an adjustment for some K-12 educators to work in a higher education environment in which the issues the students are facing outside the class can greatly impact their performance in the class.

"If someone offers you an amazing opportunity and you're not sure you can do it, say yes—then learn how to do it later." — Richard Branson

---

91   www.nationalservice.gov

Tip 4: Earn a Degree in Adult Education or Higher Education

After completing some of the aforementioned tips and other strategies, you may decide to enroll in a college program with a major and degree geared toward working with adults in higher education.[92] On the other hand, you may already have advanced degrees in your field and want to teach at a college or university. It still may be helpful to do professional development training to learn the best practices in higher education and how to facilitate teaching adult learners.

"If fear is cultivated it will become stronger, if faith is cultivated it will achieve mastery." —John Paul Jones

Tip 5: Attend Higher Education Conferences

There are many national and international conferences for professionals in higher education. The topics can range from student affairs, developmental or transitional education, advising, or discipline to retention and enrollment. Attendance can provide a great professional development opportunity to learn about the latest research in higher education as well as opportunities for networking.

"I think education is power. I think that being able to communicate with people is power. One of my main goals on the planet is to encourage people to empower themselves." — *Oprah Winfrey*

---

92   www.Capella.edu/OnlineCollege

5 Tips for Careers in the Health Care Field

Health care careers are a close cousin to higher education, with practitioners earning higher degrees to become faculty and faculty maintaining licensure in their respective health care field.

Tip 1: Research Careers in Health Care

One of the tips for entering or advancing in careers in the health care field is to research the occupation of interest to learn valuable information, such as the job description, job outlook, median salary, and work environment. According to the Bureau of Labor Statistics Occupational Outlook Handbook, employment in health care occupations is projected to grow by 19% from 2014 to 2024, much faster than the average for all occupations, adding about 2.3 million new jobs.[93]

"Anybody who succeeds is helping people. The secret to success is find a need and fill it; find a hurt and heal it; find a problem and solve it." —Robert H. Schuller

Tip 2: Identify Education Needed

If you are changing careers or would like to advance in your career in the health care field, conduct research to determine if you have the level of education needed for the career that you desire. For example, health care management is an area that may be of interest to you. To find the level of education needed for health care management, you can visit the Healthcare Management Degree Guide website.[94]

---

93 https://www.bls.gov/oco
94 www.phoenix.edu/Health/Degrees

"You can learn new things at any time in your life if you're willing to be a beginner. If you actually learn to like being a beginner, the whole world opens up to you" —Barbara Sher

Tip 3: Find the Best Match

There are numerous jobs in the health care field. Some of the jobs have been around for centuries and some are relatively new, emerging jobs. There are several websites that provide information on the best jobs in the health care field (U.S, News, The 20 Best Paying Healthcare Careers, Career Vitals, and Health Jobs Nationwide).[95] This information will help you to learn about the vast array of top occupations in the health care field. Some job search sites are general for all occupations. Other job search sites are for specific occupations such as higher education or health care. It may be helpful to use the services of both types of job search sites. The job search sites not only alert you about opening positions, but they also often provide helpful tips on interviewing, creating effective résumés, and salary negotiations.

"Health is a large word. It embraces not the body only, but the mind and spirit as well; and not today's pain or pleasure alone, but the whole being and outlook of man." —James H. West

"When health is absent Wisdom cannot reveal itself, Art cannot become manifest, Strength cannot be exerted, Wealth is useless and Reason is powerless." —Herophilies, 300 B.C.

---

95 money.usnews.com/careers/best-jobs/rankings/best-healthcare-jobs, https://superscholar.org/best-paying-jobs-health-care-not-doctor-career/, www.careervitals.com , www. UltimateMedical.edu/Management, www. iHireHealthCareAdministration.com, www.indeed.com/q-Healthcare-jobs.html

Tip 4: Try Out the Career by Volunteering

Another great way to jumpstart a new career in the health care field is to volunteer. Volunteering your services not only gets you a foot in the door of a health care establishment, but it also gives you an opportunity to learn from someone with years of experience in the field of your choice. While volunteering in the health care profession, you can learn whether or not this career path is for you and make a difference in other people's lives at the same time.[96]

"Only a life lived in the service to others is worth living." — Albert Einstein

Tip 5: Network

When exploring a new career or advancing in your current career, there is power in networking. For instance, you can do informational interviews with people who are working in an occupation that interests you. Also, when you are seeking a job, let your friends, family, and others know so they can look out for any job openings that may interest you. Health careers have a special networking website.[97]

"People who ask confidently get more than those who are hesitant and uncertain. When you've figured out what you want to ask for, do it with certainty, boldness and confidence. Don't be shy or feel intimidated by the experience. You may face some unexpected criticism, but be prepared for it with confidence."
—Jack Canfield

---

96   http://www.publichealth.org/volunteering/
97   www.nationalhealthcareerreernetwork.com

5 Tips for Self-Taught Pathways to Meaningful Careers

How do you make a meaningful career in higher education? You forge your own path.

Higher education institutions provide the formal education to students so they can earn degrees or other credentials required for specific career paths. Yet self-taught pathways to entry and promotion are replete within higher education institutions. Advertised positions within student affairs or administrative lines ask for a broadly defined mix of relevant experience and education. Once in a position, opportunities for transfers within the institution or promotions emerge with professional experience gained during one's tenure at the institution. Following are tips that offer ideas for gaining just this kind of self-taught experience.

Tip 1: Shift from a Credential-Building Orientation to a Skill- and Experience-Building One

Become aware of competent colleagues for whom you hold a deep respect who do not hold the credentials typically associated with certain positions. Use an informational interview approach to find out more about how they forged their self-taught pathway. There are many free online skill-building opportunities including Marc & Angel's *Hacklife* blogpost *12 Dozen Places to Educate Yourself Online for Free* and Kyle Pearce's *DIYGENIUS* blogpost 100+ *Self-Education Resources for Lifelong Learning Online.*[98]

> *"Self-education will make you a fortune."* —Jim Rohn

---

98   http://www.marcandangel.com/2010/11/15/12-dozen-places-to-self-educate-yourself-online/, https://www.diygenius.com/100-self-education-resources-for-lifelong-learners/

Tip 2: Take Advantage of Unique Opportunities for Self-Taught Credentialing Within Your Institution

Convocations, professional development days, the Center for Excellence in Teaching and Learning (CETL), and conferences all offer opportunities for skill building. Ensure that these required events are well worth your time by selecting at least one thing at every required event you would like to master. For example, these are the CETL offerings at the University of Indiana at Purdue and Indianapolis.[99]

> *"Life is a continuous learning process. Each day presents an opportunity for learning."* —Lailah Gifty Akita

Tip 3: Select Service Activities with Skill Building in Mind

Of all duties in higher education positions, you have the most freedom to select your service activity. Be strategic and choose an activity that will help build skills and experience. As a service activity in a previous job, I served on a grant-writing team. With no formal experience in federal grant writing, I learned on the job from others who had served as grant writers for years. I cowrote awarded federal proposals. This success opened doors for me to continue in this field, opportunities I never imagined when I began. Use the principles of SMART goal setting to strategically select your service commitments.[100]

> *"Education is not the learning of facts, but the training of the mind to think."* —Albert Einstein

---

99   https://ctl.iupui.edu/Resources
100   https://www.mindtools.com/pages/article/newHTE_90.htm

Tip 4: Reframe New Projects as Skill Building Rather Than Extra Assigned Duty

Assigned to a new committee? Use it as an opportunity to gain process management skills and tangible experience. Assigned to head up the implementation of "initiative x here" in your department? Begin with a successful end in mind by employing your particular skill set (e.g., persuasion of others, teaching strategies, detail orientation) to become a successful project manager. This Vanderbilt website suggests other strategies to identify skills and gain experience.[101]

> *"You can teach a student a lesson for a day; but if you can teach him to learn by creating curiosity, he will continue the learning process as long as he lives."* —Clay P. Bedford

Tip 5: Keep Yourself Inspired by Updating Your Résumé

Make your accomplishments visible to yourself and others by incorporating new training and projects into your résumé.[102]

> *"You cannot hope to build a better world without improving the individuals. To that end, each of us must work for his own improvement and, at the same time, share a general responsibility for all humanity, our particular duty being to aid those to whom we think we can be most useful."* —Marie Curie

---

101 https://my.vanderbilt.edu/gradcareer/non-academic-careers
102 https://www.themuse.com/advice/6-good-reasons-to-always-keep-your-resume-updated

Spotlights – Professionals Who Stay the Course

This section features professionals who have mastered the tips recommended in this book. We hope their stories and strategies inspire you.

Embracing Leadership Roles

Jacqueline Gray

Leadership can take on many roles. A person can be a leader in the church, community, job, school, politics, military, or many other facets of society. A leader has a vision and can effectively motivate others to combine their skills, talents, and experience to work together to make the vision become a reality. Achieving a college degree is often the gateway to open opportunities of leadership roles in careers. There are many organizations such as the American Association of University Women (AAUW), which, through their fellowships, grants, scholarships, and diligent hard work in local and national communities, promote women and men to embrace leadership roles. Jacqueline Gray, President of the Baltimore Branch of the AAUW, is one person who has embraced leadership roles in her career and the community.

A. Yvette Myrick (AYM): Please tell us a little bit about yourself.

Jacqueline Gray (JG): I am a native Baltimorean who attended public schools in the inner city, eventually earning a bachelor's degree from Coppin State University and later a master's degree from Johns Hopkins University. I also graduated from Georgetown University with a Certificate in International Business.

I am currently a contracts and procurement professional. After spending 20 years in private industry, managing and negotiating contracts, I am now with the federal government doing the same type of work. I have a keen interest in technology, health and wellness, music, and travel. I also love meeting people from other cultures and nationalities.

AYM: Please tell me a little bit about the American Association of University Women (AAUW).

JG: AAUW is a nonprofit organization established by women in 1881 to promote equity for women and girls through advocacy, education and research. AAUW's national headquarters is located in downtown Washington, DC. AAUW has branches of operation throughout the United States. In addition to being a champion for women's rights, AAUW takes pride in providing outreach activities at the state and local levels. Branches throughout the 50 states raise funds to provide scholarships and tuition assistance for students enrolled in colleges and universities. AAUW educates women on important issues such as equal pay, gender equity, voting awareness, and laws that affect women, their families, and their communities.

AYM: What interested you in getting involved in AAUW?

JG: While working in corporate America, I noticed there were not a lot of professional organizations that served women in business. I was invited to a women's summit one year and was approached by an AAUW member who invited me to a monthly meeting. The women at the meeting were friendly, inviting, and well organized. I liked the activities that they were involved in and I immediately joined. I am entering my 5th year as an AAUW member.

AYM: How do you think that AAUW prepares women for leadership roles?

JG: The local branches of AAUW comprise members, officers, and board members. When the terms of office for officers and board members are up, the branches look to their existing member bases to fill the vacated office positions. These positions are all on a volunteer basis, but they provide members with a chance to sharpen leadership skills by putting them in positions where they develop, shape and execute agendas, set goals and are in charge of ensuring those goals are met. Branch officers consist of a President, Vice President of Membership, Vice President of Programming, Secretary, Treasurer and a slate of board members who help the branch officers set policy and carry out the mission.

AYM: Why did you decide to take on leadership roles in your life and at AAUW?

JG: To sustain growth, longevity, and a legacy, one must always be about the business of planning, organizing, leading and controlling, and having a voice in things that matter. This is a necessary endeavor in one's private and professional life. AAUW members must not only show up at meetings, but they must also take on leadership roles to sustain and grow the organizations. That is why I chose to serve in various officer roles with AAUW. The national and local chapters have done mighty fine work over the years, and our communities need the services of groups such as AAUW. Currently, one of AAUW's requirements for becoming a member is that the applicant be a college graduate. That is because college-educated women have gained the necessary educational skills and, in most cases, the professional skills that equip them to become advocates for the rights of women and girls in our society.

AYM: Jacqueline, thank you for sharing your educational and career background. It was fascinating to learn about the great work of AAUW. I was also impressed with the AAUW campus leadership programs to shape the next generation of leaders such as its National Conference for College Women Student Leaders (NCCWSL), which unites college women from across the country to address important leadership issues of the day. For additional information about AAUW, please visit its website.[103] As you have demonstrated from your educational and career journey, achieving a higher education degree can open up opportunities to embrace career and personal leadership roles.

---

103   www.aauw.org

Thinking Outside the Border: Seeking Job Opportunities in Education Outside the United States

Chinyere Okoli and Jackée Okoli

In addition to the job opportunities in the U.S., there are opportunities to start or advance careers by working in the education field outside the U.S. You may have hurdles to consider during the job search process, including additional documentations such as a work visa, vaccination requirements, and communication issues. Nevertheless, it could be worthwhile to tackle these hurdles to learn about different cultures and languages. Furthermore, the skill set that you gain from teaching abroad could advance your career. There are hundreds of jobs in the education field, and more jobs are being created to adjust to technological advances, a global economy, diverse student populations, and scholarly contributions in the education field. To take advantage of these great job opportunities, it is important to have the skill set, training, and education needed; to be resourceful; and, sometimes, to be willing to relocate in the U.S. or outside the U.S.

This spotlight person is actually two pioneering people, Chinyere and Jackée Okoli, who have mastered the art of thinking outside the borders to take advantage of job opportunities outside the U.S. They are sisters who have made it one of their life's passions to work aboard. Chinyere graduated from Duke University in 2008 with a degree in civil engineering and a certificate in architecture. Jackée graduated from the University of Southern California in 2011 with a degree in narrative studies. Although their college degrees were in different fields and did not focus in education, both women decided to pursue jobs in teaching English outside the U.S.

Chinyere is currently teaching English in Japan; she has taught there for more than 5 years. As a result of working aboard, Chinyere became a world traveler. She has now traveled to more than 17 countries. Jackée taught English in Japan and South Korea for almost 2 years. She has returned to the United States and is currently in medical school. I had the pleasure of interviewing Chinyere and Jackée and learning about their worldly experiences from working aboard.

A. Yvette Myrick (AYM): Why did you decide to seek job opportunities outside the U.S.?

Chinyere Okoli (CO): I wanted to live abroad and learn a new language.

Jackée Okoli (JO): I wanted to work outside the U.S. because the job covered the cost of my rent and provided longer vacations. The cost of living was cheaper, and the cost of my airfare was refunded.

AYM: Do you have any tips for pursuing job opportunities in other countries?

CO: The easiest way to get a job abroad is to teach, especially English. If it is your first time abroad, I would recommend looking for programs like the JET (Japanese Exchange and Teaching) Program that can help you transition into living abroad. But be aware that some countries require you to have at least a bachelor's degree.

JO: My tip is to think outside the box. Many people teach English and love it despite the fact that teaching is not their original profession. Also, do your research before taking on a job abroad because some programs are better than others.

AYM: What are the pros and cons of working outside the U.S.?

CO: The pros are you can learn another language and culture. You can learn about yourself, such as your likes, dislikes, and personality. You will also learn how to handle different situations, cultural differences, and people from different backgrounds. It also allows you to be less judgmental of people from different cultures. The cons are you are often alone, so it can be lonely. It might be hard to make friends, especially if you are living in a big city; this makes it harder to learn the language. Another con is, sometimes, the culture shock can be too much to handle. Also, depending on the culture, you may have to deal with stereotypes or even racism.

JO: A pro is all the benefits that I mentioned. Also, you can meet wonderful people and learn a new language. In addition, it looks good on your résumé. The cons are you miss out on holidays and important events, such as birthdays, weddings, and graduations. Also, it can take a while to get adjusted due to culture shock.

AYM: Thank you for sharing your insight on working aboard. You both shared a wealth of knowledge from the tips on seeking job opportunities to the pros and cons of working aboard. It seems that seeking job opportunities abroad and working though the additional hurdles during the job search process can be an educational and rewarding adventure.

Making a Successful Transition from a K-12 Career to a Higher Education Career

Phyllis Pollard

Most educators have a passion for learning and helping others to reach their educational goals. They may decide early during their educational journey to focus on a college major for a career choice in early childhood, secondary, or postsecondary, such as adult or higher education. Then, they may start a career working as an educator, administrator, or in another capacity with students at a particular age in an elementary school, middle school, high school, college, or other academic setting. Some educators may devote a lifelong, successful career and thrive by working with students in a certain age range. Still others may devote their time by working with students of all age ranges such as our spotlight person, Phyllis Pollard. Phyllis shares her journey, describing how she was able to successfully transition from a K-12 career to a higher education career, and on to building her portfolio of working with students across different age ranges.

A.Yvette Myrick (AYM): Tell us a little about yourself.

Phyllis Pollard (PP): I have been employed in the field of education since September 1988. I've always wanted to work in a position where I can be of help to others. I spent 14 years working in the Baltimore City Public School system in various positions, such as office assistant, school secretary, high school business education teacher, and office manager. I also spent one year working in a Washington, DC Public Charter School as an administrative assistant. Oh boy, do I remember the commute, sitting in traffic on (Hwy) 295!

I began working at Coppin State University (CSU) in August 2014 after being laid off from my position as office manager at an all-boys transformation school located in West Baltimore. I currently work as an academic advisor in the First-Year Experience office. I have been employed in this position for about a year. In this position, I am able to establish and build relationships with students as they grow and develop in their educational plans and goals. Prior to working as an academic advisor, I worked as an executive administrative assistant to the Vice President of Enrollment Management at Coppin. I remember attending summer camp at Coppin (then Coppin College), as I grew up in West Baltimore, just walking distance from Coppin. Coppin has a high school on its campus, Coppin Academy. It is nice to see the students, in their uniforms, as they walk across campus. Some of the students are dually enrolled and take courses at CSU. Coppin has a brand new state-of-the-art science and technology building and an excellent nursing program; however, the campus still struggles (as do other local universities) with low enrollment.

AYM: Why did you decide on a career in K-12?

PP: I decided on a career in K-12 after completing an application for employment in Baltimore City. I was in my early to mid-20s and looked forward to working in a school setting. At the time, I had no idea I would be embarking on a career in education and returning to my former high school as a business education teacher and office manager.

I enjoyed working in the K-12 setting, interacting with the students and staff. Of course, being employed as a 12-month employee, my summers (without summer school) were pretty quiet, and I always looked forward to winter and spring breaks!

AYM: Why did you decide on a career in higher education?

PP: After working in K-12 for so many years, I sought positions in higher education. After completing my master's degree in education, I thought about teaching on the college level. I just wanted to get my foot in the door and decide in which area I wanted to work.

AYM: What do you think are differences and similarities between the two?

PP: There are several differences between K-12 and higher education. For example, in higher education, students pay for their courses through grants, scholarships, student loans, and parental support. Most college students are initially placed in courses as a result of placement testing. College students choose courses that are under the program in which they are studying. On the other hand, in K-12 education (public education), classes are free. When students reach high school, they are responsible for paying class dues to help offset expenses such as graduation, farewell, ring dance, prom, class trips, and the like. In K-12 education, students are required to take exams and tests such as Partnership for Assessment of Readiness for College and Careers (PARCC) and high school assessment exams. Students follow a schedule of classes and consult with a guidance counselor regarding certain courses as they get close to graduation.

Similarly, parental support is present in both K-12 and higher education. Freshman students have parental support as they begin to take college classes and throughout the freshman year. Typically, upper level students do not have the parental support present on campus because it is not needed. At this stage most upper level students are familiar with programs and procedures. They are considered young adults who can take care of their personal business and needs.

AYM: What are some ways that we can build the connection between K-12 and higher education?

PP: Some ways to build the connection between K-12 and higher education are the following:

- Dual enrollment programs with local high schools

- 5-week summer bridge programs (for incoming freshman students) to introduce them to higher education

Coppin State University offers such a program called Student Academic Success Academy (SASA). Students remain on campus for 5 weeks. They attend classes such as freshman seminar, English I, technology fluency, and developmental math and reading courses to prepare them for classes offered in their major program. They are introduced to various resources available to them; this helps them with adjusting to college life and being away from home. Local freshman students are also eligible to participate in SASA. When the program ends, students are registered for fall courses, having acquired a few credits ahead of other students in their graduation cohort.

AYM: Phyllis, thank you for sharing your journey from working in various roles in K-12 to higher education. By working with all age ranges, you are doing something that has been galvanizing the education system to increase college enrollment and completion. Most stakeholders realize the power in K-12 and higher education partnering together to build a stronger education system for a global economy. As you mentioned, some high school students enroll in college courses to complete dual enrollment programs. Also, some college professors provide professional development training so that the K-12 high school teachers can teach the college courses at their high schools. Some K-12 educators also simultaneously teach college courses or work in other roles in higher education. More and more professionals are choosing career pathways in education that bridge K-12 and higher education. Whether you choose a career in K-12, higher education or both, strive to make a positive difference in others, as well as yourself.

Integrating Higher Education Careers Into Integrative Health Care

Dr. Gabrielle Julien-Molineaux

As a higher education professional, there are numerous pathways that one can take to lead to a meaningful, rewarding career. Although many higher education professionals may choose to work at colleges and universities, others may choose to use their education and skill sets in other career fields. One career field that has provided numerous opportunities for higher education professionals is the health care field. An area in the health care field that may not come to mind as quickly as a Western or traditional medical care area is a career in integrative health care. Nevertheless, incorporating higher education careers into integrative health care is becoming a viable career pathway.

Dr. Gabrielle Julien-Molineaux is a prime example of a higher education professional that has chosen integrative health care as an avenue to thrive in a higher education career. Dr. Julien-Molineaux was born and raised in Trinidad, but she has lived in the United States for almost 30 years. She grew up in a family of nurses. Her mother was a nurse, a nursing administrator at a hospital, and a teacher in a nursing school. Nevertheless, Dr. Julien-Molineaux did not set out for a career in nursing or the health care field. In fact, she was a journalism major in college. But becoming a journalist as a full-time career was not in the cards for Dr. Julien-Molineaux.

Dr. Julien-Molineaux's involvement in integrative health care began through the use of *reiki* as a form of personal self-care. The U.S. Department of Health and Human Services defines reiki as "a complementary health approach in which practitioners place their hands lightly on or just above a person, with the goal of facilitating the person's own healing response." Dr. Julien-Molineaux describes reiki as one of the "several modalities under the umbrella of integrative health." She lists some of the uses of reiki: stress and pain relief, pre- and post-operative comfort, and deep relaxation.

A culmination of her interests in higher education and integrative health care led to the decision to write her dissertation on the study of enrollment management and universities that specialize in complementary medicine and integrative health care. Dr. Julien-Molineaux completed her dissertation as part of the Graduate School of Education and Human Development doctoral program at The George Washington University. As a result of her research, her dissertation has made a significant contribution to the field of integrative health care.

There are many other ways that higher education and integrative health care can be bridged to create a viable career. For example, Dr. Julien-Molineaux pointed out that "many large institutions such as The George Washington University have integrative health centers where medical students can study cases alongside integrative health practitioners, such as naturopathic physicians." Additionally, she mentioned that some nurses at large institutions like Johns Hopkins Hospital have been trained in reiki.

Incorporating a higher education career into integrative health care is an excellent opportunity to get involved in a dynamic and growing health care field. A few career opportunities for a higher education professional in integrative health care include enrollment management, teaching, administration, or consulting. More importantly, not only can integrative health care be advantageous as a career, but the study and application of its techniques also can be advantageous to the mind and body of a higher education professional.

Self-Taught Pathways to Higher Education

Eva Young

Sometimes we select career pathways that are structured; therefore, we are able to effortlessly stay on the straight and narrow path to reach the desired career outcome. Sometimes we select career pathways involving many exits and entrances along the path, as life happens on the road to the desired career outcome. Other times we create our own career pathways paved with the skills, education, training, and talents that we accumulate along the way. The spotlight person who embodies the drive and direction needed to create a self-taught pathway to higher education is Eva Young. Ms. Young was able to make the most of education and training to create a career pathway that is a valuable commodity.

Eva Young developed her own career path into Information technology (IT). While enrolled in a graduate program in chemistry, she served as a research assistant developing a biocatalysis degradation database. [Eva explains to all of us in the audience who are not biochemists that this refers to the process of speeding up chemical reactions with natural bacteria for the purpose of hastening the degradation of pollutants such as herbicides]. During her work on this project, she became adept at several Web tools including html, and then one thing led to another. She joined the University of Minnesota's Policy Office in 1997 and for the last two decades has worked on projects and attended conferences that enable her to continue to hone her IT skills. She has mastered Access, ColdFusion (a rapid Web application development platform), and most recently Drupal (open source software for Web content management).

When she entered her position at the Policy Office, she wanted to learn how to administer a Web server. So she set about doing just that. When first introduced to the ColdFusion Web application development platform, she thought it looked quite interesting. She took a ColdFusion course at the university and became convinced of its potential for the Policy Office. With that knowledge, she convinced her supervisor to invest in ColdFusion. She jumped in to intentionally utilize the software intensively across a broad range of projects for the Policy Office. And as a result, she became an adroit user of ColdFusion. Combining her work with ColdFusion and her work with Access, she has reached a high level of proficiency with data structures such as SQL (Structured Query Language) server databases.

The opportunity to develop skills on the job has also allowed Eva to develop marketable skills of value to other higher education institutions. At the Policy Office, Drupal replaced ColdFusion. Working with a Drupal consultant, Eva implemented the shift to Drupal. After completing this project she was so adept that another university hired her as a Drupal consultant.

Choosing a self-taught career path enabled Eva to shape her own job description. Indeed, it has been an unwritten part of her job description: From the first day, Eva has had to figure out what to do and how to do it without a clear written set of guidelines or precedence. Eva embraced this challenge. Pursuing a self-taught career path has provided a daily opportunity to infuse her career in higher education with meaning.

Questions for Reflection

1. Do you think that leadership roles in higher education are different from other leadership? Why or why not?

2. Reflect on a leadership role that you currently have or would like to have. What five things will you do to excel in the role?

3. What are the differences among job searches for K-12, higher education, nonprofit educational organizations, or for-profit educational businesses?

4. What three things will let you know whether a job may or may not be a good fit for you?

5. Why do you think some people focus only on a career in K-12 or a career in higher education?

6. In what ways can the two fields, K-12 and higher education, intermingle as career pathways?

7. In what ways can the two fields, higher education and health care, intermingle as career pathways?

8. What are the top five skills that you have attained from your previous or current jobs?

9. If you were to create your own career pathway, what qualifications, skills, and education would be needed to excel in a job for that career pathway?

10. Which career pathways do you think will be obsolete in the next 10 years? Which career pathways do you think will be thriving in the next 10 years?

My Higher Education Journal

Please use this space to respond and reflect on the ideas presented in this chapter for your own professional growth.

7

Self-Care

Introduction

SELF-CARE IS NOT being selfish. We all felt called to higher education and keeping that calling front and center is the key to attaining a meaningful career in higher education. Key to keeping your original purpose in the forefront is taking proper care of yourself.

> *"This is the true joy in life, the being used for a purpose recognized by yourself as a mighty one." —George Bernard Shaw*

5 Tips for Self-Care

A personal mission statement is one way of presenting a short and compelling daily reminder to yourself of your purpose in higher education. Nelson Mandela's mission statement shows the power of a few words to guide the day's actions and one's future aspirations.

"End Apartheid." —Nelson Mandela

Tip 1: Never Lose Sight of Your Original Mission

Adapt one of the formats below to create a statement that describes your core purpose in a convincing manner (Constandse, n.d.). Then, find a way to effectively remind yourself daily of your mission statement (e.g., read it out loud first thing in the morning; ubiquitously post it in your car, bathroom, desk, kitchen, door; send it in a daily email reminder).

"To...[what you want to achieve, do or become]...so that...[reasons why it is important], I will do this by...[specific behaviors or actions you can use to get there]."

"I value...[choose one to three values/character traits]...because... [reasons why these values are important to you]. Accordingly, I will... [what you can do to live by these values]."[104]

"To develop and cultivate the qualities of...[two to three values/character traits]...that I admire in ...[an influential person in your life]...so that...[why you want to develop these qualities], I will...[what you will do]."

"Let the first act of every morning be to make the following resolve for the day: I shall not fear anyone on Earth. I shall fear only God. I shall not bear ill will toward anyone. I shall not submit to injustice from anyone. I shall conquer untruth by truth. And in resisting untruth, I shall put up with all suffering."
—Mahatma Ghandi – Daily Resolution

---

104   http://www.timethoughts.com/goalsetting/ListOfSampleValues.htm

Tip 2: Spend Your Time Doing Things and
Having Thoughts That Are Important but Not Urgent

The things most important in life—one's purpose, core relationships, essential values, and oneself—flourish when maintained proactively. The more of our lives we spend doing those things, with those people, and thinking those thoughts that are most important to us while taking good care of ourselves, the more in balance we feel. When we spend time on things that are unimportant, we pay a big price. Not only do we squeeze time and energy from our core but we also spend less time nurturing our core, thereby bringing unpleasant and urgent repercussions that require a response. Neglecting one's family creates severe family tensions. Inadequate sleep and relaxation, poor nutrition, and a sedentary lifestyle collectively lead to poor health outcomes. Neglecting one's own work to work on the priorities of others fuels resentment.

"It is not a daily increase, but a daily decrease. Hack away at the inessentials." —Bruce Lee

Although such a situation is an occupational hazard in higher education, it is not inevitable. Steven Covey's *Seven Habits of Highly Effective People* (Covey, 1989) includes a time-management tool to ensure that we do not sacrifice the important things in the name of pursuing the unimportant ones. Adapted in the table below, Covey divides all activities into four categories. The table is divided top to bottom by importance; important activities are on the top. The table is divided left to right by urgency. A meaningful life in balance is spent proactively investing in one's life's purpose, relationships, and self-care while living a life consistent with one's core values (*non-urgent and important*). The tool prompts us to aim to remain in or return to the non-urgent and important quadrant to achieve our balance.

Careers in higher education include daily requests from others requesting immediate follow-up (*unimportant and urgent*). The number of items in the inbox inevitably exceeds the hours in a day, but our commitments to the institution, discipline, and our high standards for ourselves, propel us to try to respond to every request despite this. To respond to these requests, we sacrifice the time most important to us, taking time from our own work in higher education, our families, and caring for ourselves. This creates a destructive dynamic where we stray again and again from the purpose we find most dear to fulfill the requests of others, leaving us feeling overworked and under-acknowledged. Neglecting the people and things most important, including ourselves, always brings repercussions. Inspired professionals become burned out. Healthy marriages fall apart. Failure to practice self-care results in poor mental or physical health.

There are several effective alternatives to saying yes to every request. Some tasks can be delegated to others. Delaying your response for 24 hours allows you to prioritize the request and think of an appropriate response. Reminding yourself that everyone says no to requests allows you to turn down requests. Perhaps the biggest strategy lies in reducing the standards for quality and timeliness we set for ourselves. Do not let the perfect be the enemy of the good enough.

A final category includes those activities that are both unimportant and non-urgent. Remind yourself that time is finite. When you say yes to something unimportant you are saying no to something important.

Using Steven Covey's matrix, plan your next day so that you intentionally choose to spend your time investing in those aspects of your life that are most important to you. Look closely at the items on the calendar; which are urgent but unimportant to you? Ask yourself these questions: Can I get out of this task? Delegate this task? What can I do with what I have now and avoid spending more time? Write a "stop saying yes to this request" note to yourself. And beware of the distant elephant. We have a strong temptation to say yes to requests for events far in the future. But when the elephant is close at hand, it is unwieldy.

"Without reflection, we go blindly on our way, creating more unintended consequences, and failing to achieve anything useful." —Margaret J. Wheatley

Engage in daily self-reflection to give more insight in getting to the important and non-urgent quadrant. What activities are so satisfying that they do not require outside acknowledgement? Which environments are most nurturing? What aspects of the day energize you? Which are most draining? Using the insight gained from your reflection, take every opportunity to choose meaningful over meaningless. Choosing a service activity? Volunteer for the committees tasked with goals you share. Love teaching more than research? Do research on the science of teaching. Make well-informed, deliberative choices to prioritize the way you use your time.

URGENT and IMPORTANT	NON-URGENT and IMPORTANT
Reaction to crises created when insufficient attention is given to your core/self-care while it is not yet urgent. • Burnout • Strained relationships • Poor mental or physical health *By avoiding the unimportant, you avoid having to respond to crises.*	Proactive investment in: • A meaningful profession • Core relationships • Healthy mind, body, and spirit *Strive to stay here.*
URGENT and UNIMPORTANT Requests from others or standards for yourself that are not consistent with your important aspects. • Email, calls, texts • Requests to participate in activity outside your job desired description *Just say no. Delegate. Delay. Decrease your standards.*	NON-URGENT and UNIMPORTANT • Trifling people • Trifling thoughts • Trifling activities *"I can resist anything but temptation."* — **Oscar Wilde** *Avoid.*

Tip 3: Managing Interruptions

Here we are referring to both interruptions by others (email, text) and self-interruptions (Facebook). One effective strategy is called the *pomodoro*.[105] Developed by Francesco Cirillo to add discipline to his study time, the pomodoro helps you be more effective by working in a manner consistent with your brain's effectiveness. You can try it:

- Pick a short task that can be completed in 25 minutes.

- Turn email and phone off and close your door.

- Set a timer for 25 minutes and start.

- Self-interruption? Jot it down and bring your focus back.

- When timer rings, mark # of distractions.

- Take a 3-5 minute break to rest your mind (not email, but deep breathing or quick walk).

- After your fourth pomodoro, take a 15-30 minute break.

"Other people's interruptions of your work are relatively insignificant compared with the countless times you interrupt yourself." —Brendan Francis

Tip 4: Setting SMART Goals

Parkinson, a British civil servant wrote that "work expands to fill the time available for its completion" in a 1955 article in the *Economist*. By setting a firm start and end time to each day, you force time to be the

---

105   Henry, A. (2014). Productivity 101: A primer to the Pomodoro technique. Retrieved from https://lifehacker.com/productivity-101-a-primer-to-the-pomodoro-technique-1598992730

master of the task. This means that you both prioritize the tasks and manage the scope of any task. Always ask yourself, "How comprehensive and detailed can I be in the time I have available?" When considering a task, think in terms of SMART goals (specific, meaningful, achievable, reflected upon, and time-bound). By thinking SMART, you are mindful of the balance between something that is realistic in the time available, but still meaningful in terms of your criteria for importance.

Turning SMART Goals into SMART Habits: Reflection log and action plan

Self-Assessment

Using Covey's important-urgent quadrant, review your activities from the previous day. Identify unimportant activities you think you can eliminate.

Setting a SMART Goal

Set a SMART goal to eliminate the unimportant activity. It should be specific (5 Ws, who, what, when, where, why), achieve a meaningful outcome, be feasible given the time and effort available, and have a deadline within the next 2 weeks.

Reflect and Revise

Review your progress toward your goal. Focusing *exclusively* on those things that are under your control, explain what you did to reach your SMART goal/prevent yourself from reaching your SMART goal. If the goal is still meaningful, revise the goal to overcome your challenges and repeat.

Tip 5: Changing Stressful Thoughts

The types of thoughts that lead to stress are repeated and negative—they are called ANTS (automatic negative thoughts). Recognizing them is the first step to challenging them. The wisdom of combating ANTS comes from a one-two punch delivered by cognitive psychology and mindfulness. Much much more on these powerful and research-based strategies is a google search away. A great guide to both is Bourne's Anxiety and Phobia Workbook; the specific techniques summarized here are adapted from his workbook.[106]

"As a single footstep will not make a path on the earth, so a single thought will not make a pathway in the mind. To make a deep physical path, we walk again and again. To make a deep mental path, we must think over and over the kind of thoughts we wish to dominate our lives." —Henry David Thoreau

Types of ANTS (Automatic Negative Thoughts):

- **Overgeneralization:** Coming to a general conclusion based on a single event, conversation or piece of evidence. These thoughts generally include "always" or "never".

  » Example: I forgot to finish the project on time. I *never* manage to do things right.

- **Filtering**: Concentrating on the negatives while ignoring the positives. Ignoring important information that contradicts one's negative view of the situation.

---

106 https://books.google.com/books/about/The_Anxiety_and_Phobia_Work-book.html?id=d3eYG3WKBs8C&printsec=frontcover&source=kp_read_button#v=onepage&q&f=false

» Example: I know my boss said most of my submission was great, but he also said there were a number of mistakes that had to be corrected...he must think I'm really hopeless.

- **All or nothing thinking**: Thinking in black and white terms (e.g., Things are right or wrong, good or bad). A tendency to view things at the extreme with no middle ground.

  » Example: I made so many mistakes.... If I can't do it perfectly, I might as well not bother.

- **Personalizing**: Taking responsibility for something that is not your fault. Thinking that what people say or do is some kind of reaction to you, or is in some way related to you.

  » Example: It is obvious she doesn't like me; otherwise, she would've said hello.

- **Catastrophizing:** Overestimating the chances of disaster. Expecting something unbearable or intolerable to happen. Such thoughts often begin with "What if...?"

  » Example: If I don't do well today, I will never get it.

- **Emotional reasoning**: Mistaking feelings for facts. Negative things you feel about yourself are held to be true because they feel true.

  » Example: I feel like a failure; therefore, I am a failure.

- **Mind reading**: Making assumptions about other people's thoughts, feelings, and behaviors without checking the evidence.

  » Example: I could tell he thought I was stupid during the interview.

- **Fortune telling error**: Anticipating an outcome or assuming your prediction is an established fact. These negative expectations can be self-fulfilling: Predicting what we would do on the basis of past behavior may prevent the possibility of change.

  » Example: It's not going to work out, so there's not much point even trying.

- **Should statements**: Using *should*, *ought*, or *must* statements can set up unrealistic expectations of yourself and others. It involves operating by rigid rules and not allowing for flexibility.

  » Example: I shouldn't feel nervous before an exam.

- **Magnification/minimization**: A tendency to exaggerate the importance of negative information or experiences, while trivializing or reducing the significance of positive information or experiences.

  » Example: He noticed I spilled something on my shirt. I know he said he will go out with me again, but I'll bet he doesn't call.

Challenging and Overcoming ANTS Is a Two-step Process

First, identify ANTS as you have them, ask yourself:

Assessment

> What is going through my mind?
> What category of ANT is it?

Diagnosis

> What is it about this situation that is upsetting me?

Step 1: Challenge Your Thoughts

Thoughts are *not* facts: Just because I think something doesn't mean it's true.

Look for Evidence

What's the evidence for and against my thought?

Am I focusing on the negatives and ignoring other information?

Am I jumping to conclusions without looking at all the facts?

Search for Alternative Explanations

- Are there any other possible explanations?

- Is there another way of looking at this?

- How would someone else think if they were in this situation?

- Am I being too inflexible in my thinking?

Put thoughts into Perspective

- Is it as bad as I am making out? What is the worst that could happen? How likely is it that the worst will happen? Even if it did happen, would it really be that bad? What could I do to get through it?

Step 2: Replace with more helpful thoughts

- Is this thought helpful? What can I say to myself that will help me remain calmer and help me achieve what I want to achieve in this situation?

- Create a positive affirmation to refute the thought. Use the 7:1 ratio. Repeat the positive affirmation seven times for every negative thought.

Referring to the list of ANT categories, generate examples of your most common ANTS, identify the category of ANT and briefly describe the event or person associated with the ANT. Now look at the list of strategies to challenge your ANT and develop questions to ask yourself to challenge your ANT. Finally, replace your original thought with a thought that will be more effective in helping you reach your goals and perform to your maximum capacity.

Thought	ANT category	Provoking event/person	Challenge the ANT	Replace with helpful thought

Resources: Four Relaxation Strategies

Abdominal Breathing

Abdominal breathing means breathing fully from your abdomen or from the bottom of your lungs. It is exactly the reverse of the way you breathe when you're anxious or tense, which is typically shallow and high in your chest. If you're breathing from your abdomen, you can place your hand on your abdomen and see it actually rise each time you inhale.

To practice abdominal breathing, follow these steps:

1. Rest your hands along the bottom of your rib cage, so that the fingertips of each hand are just touching.

2. Inhale slowly and deeply through your nose into the bottom of your lungs. Your chest should move only slightly, while your stomach rises, pushing your hands up. Your fingertips should move apart slightly as you breathe in. To help you breathe slowly, you can count slowly to 4 or 5; do not take in big gulps of air all at once.

    • When you've inhaled fully, pause for a moment, holding your breath.

    • Then exhale fully through your mouth or nose. As you exhale, just let yourself go and imagine your entire body going loose and limp. Focus attention on exhaling slowly and evenly, rather than all at once. Your fingertips should come together again as your lungs empty.

    • You can use a calming phrase as you breathe out, such as *relax*, or *let go*. As you practice your breathing, this calming phrase becomes associated with the relaxing breathing exercise and it alone can produce calming feelings.

- To fully relax, take and release 10 abdominal breaths.

- If you feel lightheaded, stop for 15-20 seconds, then start again.

- By practicing 5 minutes per day for 2 weeks, you will start to feel its effect and can use it both proactively (for generalized stress reduction), preventively (prior to a stressful event), and reactively in the moment of stress itself.

Source: Adapted from Bourne, E. (2015). *The anxiety and phobia workbook*. Oakland, CA: New Harbinger Publications.

Progressive Muscle Relaxation

Focus your attention on trying not to tense muscles other than the specific group at each step. This is very difficult at first, so just do your best. Don't hold your breath or grit your teeth. Breathe slowly and evenly and think only about the tension-relaxation contrast. Each tensing is for 7-10 seconds; each relaxing 15-20 seconds. Count "1,000 2,000..." until you have a feel for the time span.

1. **Breathing.** Take three deep abdominal breaths. Say your calming phrase as you exhale.

2. **Hands**. The fists are tensed; relaxed. As you relax, use your calming phrase. Focus your attention on feeling the buildup and releasing of tension.

3. **Biceps.** The biceps are tensed (make a muscle, but shake your hands to make sure you're not tensing them into a fist); relaxed (drop your arms to the chair; really drop them).

4. **Triceps.** The triceps are tensed (extend your arms out straight and lock your elbows, bend your arms the wrong way); relaxed (drop them).

5. **Forehead.** Tense the muscles in your forehead by raising your eyebrows as far as you can; relax. Imagine your forehead muscles becoming smooth and limp as they relax.

6. **Eyes.** Close your eyes tightly; relax. Imagine sensations of deep relaxation spreading all around the area of your eyes.

7. **Jaw.** The mouth is opened as far as possible; relaxed. Let your lips part and allow your jaw to hang loose.

8 **Neck (lateral).** With the shoulders straight and relaxed, turn the head slowly to the right, as far as you can; relax. Turn to the left; relax. Try to visualize the muscle group being tensed.

9. **Neck (forward).** Dig your chin into your chest; relax.

10. **Shoulders.** Tighten your shoulders by raising them as if you were going to touch your ears. Hold. Then relax. Release your muscles abruptly; then relax, enjoying the sudden feeling of limpness.

11. **Chest**. Take as deep a breath as possible; then take a little more. Hold for up to 10 seconds; then release slowly. Imagine any excess tension in your chest flowing away with the exhalation.

12. **Stomach**: Tighten your stomach muscles by sucking your stomach in. Imagine a wave of relaxation spreading through your abdomen.

13. **Buttocks**. Tense the buttocks by pulling them together tightly and raise pelvis slightly off chair; relax.

14. **Thighs**. Extend legs and raise them about 6 inches off the floor or the footrest, but don't tense the stomach; relax. Dig your feet (heels) into the floor or footrest; relax.

15. **Calves**. Point the feet up as far as possible (beware of cramps— if you feel them coming on, shake loose); relax.

16. **Toes**. With legs relaxed, dig your toes into the floor; relax. Bend the toes up as far as possible; relax.

17. **Review**. Mentally scan your body for any residual tension. If a particular area remains tense, repeat one or two tense-relax cycles for that group of muscles.

18. **Experience**: Now imagine a wave of relaxation slowly spreading throughout your body, starting at your head and gradually penetrating every muscle group all the way down to your toes.

19. **Practice**: Initially, it will take 20-30 minutes to practice this exercise. Over time, you will get more efficient and it will reduce to 15-20 minutes. You can tape your instructions to yourself.

20. **Focus**: After you've become an expert on your tension areas (after a few weeks), you can concern yourself only with those and skip the muscles that are not a problem for you. These exercises will not eliminate tension, but when it arises, you will know it immediately, and you will be able to "tense-relax" or even simply wish it away.

The Peaceful Scene

After deep abdominal breathing and progressive muscle relaxation, visualizing a peaceful scene can promote a global sense of relaxation and free you from anxious thoughts. As with deep breathing and muscle relaxation, once practiced, you can benefit from the power of association that a brief reminder of the peaceful scene will bring.

Example One:

You're walking along a beautiful, deserted beach. You are barefoot and can feel the firm white sand beneath your feet as you walk along the margin of the sea. You can hear the sound of the surf as the waves ebb and flow. The sound is hypnotic, relaxing you more and more. The water is a beautiful turquoise blue flecked with whitecaps far out where the waves are cresting. Near the horizon you can see a small sailboat gliding smoothly along. The sound of the waves breaking on the shore lulls you deeper and deeper into relaxation. You draw in the fresh, salty smell of the air with each breath. Your skin glows with the warmth of the sun. You can feel a gentle breeze against your cheek and ruffling your hair. Taking in the whole scene, you feel very calm and at ease.

Example Two:

Now picture yourself snuggled in your sleeping bag. Daylight is breaking in the forest. You can feel the rays of the sun beginning to warm your face. The dawn sky stretches above you in pastel shades of pink and orange. You can smell the fresh, piney fragrance of the surrounding woods. Nearby you can hear the rushing waters of a mountain stream. The crisp, cool morning air is refreshing and invigorating. You're feeling very cozy, comfortable, and secure.

The goal is to create a scene (real or imaginary, such as floating on a cloud) that you can visualize in such great detail that it captures your total attention. Your peaceful scene should contain references to the sights, sounds, smells, and feels of the scene to allow yourself to be transported to the scene.

Answer the following questions to create your scene: What does the scene look like? What colors are prominent? What sounds are present? What time of day is it? What is the temperature? What are you touching or in physical contact with in the scene? What does the air smell like? Are you alone or with somebody else?

You can tape the peaceful scene so that it is played immediately after your progressive muscle relaxation.

Meditation

Meditation brings you into the present, absorbs your attention in the here and now rather than thinking about the past or future. Meditation involves the absence of thought or feeling. The repetition and absorptive focus on one thing induces the meditative state.

- Find as quiet an environment as possible. If not silent, play something with soft instrumental or nature sounds (e.g., ocean waves).
- Reduce muscle tension through progressive muscle relaxation of the upper portion of your body (head, neck, shoulders). Add the following exercises:
  » Slowly touch your chin to your chest three times.
  » Bend your head back to gently stretch the back of your neck three times.
  » Bend your head over to your right shoulder three times.
  » Bend your head over to your left shoulder three times.
  » Slowly rotate your head clockwise for three complete rotations.

» Slowly rotate your head counterclockwise for three complete rotations.

- Sitting pose

  » Eastern style: cross-legged on the floor with a pillow supporting your buttocks. Rest your hands on your thighs. Lean slightly forward so that some of your weight is supported by your thighs and buttocks.

  » Western style: Sit in a comfortable straight-backed chair, with your feet on the floor and legs uncrossed, hands on your thighs.

- Other notes:

  » Keep your back and neck straight without straining to do so. Do not assume a tight, inflexible posture. If you need to scratch or move, do so.

  » You might fall asleep if you lie down or support your head. You can meditate outside your daily practice to help you fall asleep.

  » It is easier if you don't do it on a full stomach or when tired.

  » You can close your eyes.

- Initially, start meditating for 5 minutes, building up to 20-30 minutes in the first month. You can build up slowly over time to an hour.

- Like all deep relaxation, you must do this every day. Five minutes is sufficient for a positive impact if it is done daily.

- Assume a nonjudgmental passive attitude.

  » Concentrate on whatever you've chosen as an object of meditation but don't force or strain yourself to do so. When thoughts or daydreams come to your mind, attempt neither to hold on to them nor to reject them too vigorously. Just allow them to come and go. Think of it as watching leaves float by on the surface of a stream.

» When your attention wanders, gently bring it back. Distractions are normal; don't judge yourself.

» Don't dwell on the outcome of your meditation. Some meditations will feel good, some mediocre, and sometimes it may be difficult to meditate at all.

» The more you let go and refrain from trying to do anything other than gently guiding your attention back to your object of focus, the deeper your experience will be.

- Select a focus for your attention (breathing, a meaningful mantra, or a physical object (picture, candle flame))

- Example meditation session using a mantra:

  » Select a meaningful word or phrase:

    ▪ Neutral word: e.g., "One"

    ▪ A Sanskrit mantra: e.g., "Om Shanti"

    ▪ Phrase of personal significance: e.g., "Let go, let God." or "I am at peace."

  » Do abdominal breathing; repeat the phrase at each exhale.

Spotlights – Professionals Who Stay the Course

This section features professionals who have mastered the tips recommended in this book. We hope their stories and strategies inspire you.

Time Management Strategies for Work-Life Balance

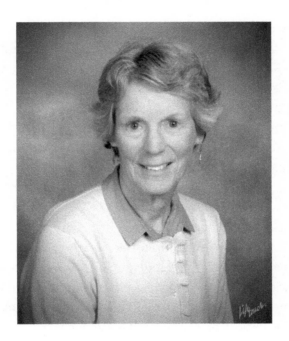

Rudi Horner

Rudi Horner's professional experience includes serving as a proposal developer, writer, and grant administrator for several higher education institutions. She is in an occupation with tight deadlines and information coming in at the last minute. To prepare applications and administer grants, she must bring together teams over which she has no direct authority, making her position just the type that leads to working overtime.

But don't call Rudi after 4:30; she won't be there. Don't email her after hours; she has no email access at home. How does she manage a perfect work–life balance? Rudi explains:

> I make sure that communication is productive. If it is a very simple and short message, I use email. If I start going back and forth, I stop losing time by picking up the phone.
>
> In terms of communication, I use several strategies to minimize nonwork conversation. I use the lunch hour as a time to socialize, and I control the time of my entry and departure. When a colleague stops by, I listen carefully to ascertain their goal for the conversation. When I hear a complaint, I strive to deflect rather than delve in. When the goal is to chit-chat, I listen for a moment, then move to summarize. I also shut my door when I face an immediate deadline.
>
> At the end of each day, I make a list of priorities for the next day. I actually put them on the calendar with a start and stop time. I purposely overestimate the time it takes to complete a task than I actually think it will take to leave time for unexpected hiccups. I also leave room between each task. In this time in between, I do email and make phone calls. At the end of the day, I prioritize again. I make a very conscious effort not to overbook myself.
>
> Overall, I pay close attention to any feelings of stress or being overworked, and I set out to do something about it. I ask for help or delegate a task. I ask my supervisor to help prioritize or delay a due date.

Thrive in Self-Care to Thrive in Higher Education

Dr. Monica Walker

For higher education educators, maintaining a meaningful, lifelong career requires self-care. This spotlight is on Dr. Monica Walker because she embodies a higher education educator who thrives professionally and personally through self-care.

Dr. Walker has 20 years of experience in higher education, significantly marked with her leadership roles and accomplishments in student success. Monica Walker, EdD, is the Dean of Developmental Education and Special Academic Programs at the Community College of Baltimore County (CCBC) in Maryland. She serves as the chief advisor in the administration of developmental education, academic pathways, library services, honors program, learning communities, academic development, culturally responsive teaching, high school collaborations, academic support, and tutoring. Prior to this appointment, she held posts as department chair and associate professor of English and coordinator for developmental writing and learning communities at CCBC and as an English instructor and assistant to the vice president for learning at Howard Community College and Anne Arundel Community College, respectively.

Dr. Walker has been honored by the League for Innovation in the Community College and the North American Council for Staff, Program, and Organizational Development. She is passionate in her commitment to the community college mission and the completion agenda. She holds a Bachelor of Science from James Madison University, a Master of Public Administration from the University of Baltimore, and a Doctorate of Education in Community College Leadership from Morgan State University.

Dr. Walker provided some tips on managing a successful higher education career through managing self-care. "The expectations and demands are growing, and leaders are expected to assume more responsibilities in their various roles," Dr. Walker said. Therefore, self-care is vitally important to meet the growing expectations and demands of a career in higher education.

First, she stressed not focusing on balance and perfection, for in her view, they are unrealistic. Instead, Dr. Walker focuses on alignment and excellence with a purpose in mind. Her purpose is connected to her personal values and mission, and she endeavors to help others to achieve their goals and best quality of life, especially through higher education. To stay true to her purpose, anything that is not in alignment with her purpose or serves as a distraction "comes off the table," Dr. Walker said. Also, it is "okay to say no" to things that are outside the alignment or are not purposeful.

Second, Dr. Walker strives to do her best and focus on excellence.

She is realistic that there may be mistakes along the way; however, as she pointed out, "you learn from the mistakes, and it is part of the process."

Another tip that Dr. Walker provided is the need to "check in with ourselves." One way that she checks in with herself is making sure that she is healthy in body, mind, and spirit. Dr. Walker stays healthy physically by being active through daily exercises such as walking, aerobics, or Pilates. Staying active helps to minimum her stressors and, at the same time, builds a foundation for a healthy lifestyle.

For the next tip, Dr. Walker reinforced the need to get a life beyond focusing primarily on careers. For example, Dr. Walker has added fulfillment to her life by being active in her community. She enjoys giving back and likes to contribute to the community through volunteer service. She believes that by giving back and helping others, she does not take herself too seriously, and it helps to make a positive difference in the community.

Last, as an essential component of self-care and wellbeing, she supports the need to make sure that relationships are strong. Dr. Walker believes that it is imperative to find the time to reach out to loved ones and to show appreciation for them. One way that she maintains a strong relationship with a loved one and, at the same time, gives back to the community is through volunteering at her daughter's elementary school.

The self-care tips provided by Dr. Walker are applicable to anyone in higher education as well as transferable to any occupation. Her wealth of knowledge has been gleaned from years of personal and professional experience. As Dr. Walker demonstrates, self-care is necessary to achieve successful, meaningful, lifelong service in higher education.

Never Lose Sight of Your Mission

Maria Paz Esguerra

Originally from California and the first in her family to attend college, Maria Paz Esguerra chose Oberlin College on the suggestion of her high school guidance counselor. After completing her bachelor's degree at Oberlin, she moved on to get her master's degree from the University of Minnesota. She received her PhD in history from the University of Michigan at Ann Arbor in 2013. She returned to Oberlin as visiting faculty in 2013-14 and spent 2014-15 as a postdoctoral fellow at the University of Illinois. During her postdoctoral fellowship, she began the process of rewriting her dissertation into a book by setting up the timeline and structure for the book and writing the book proposal. She also used the postdoctoral fellowship to gain additional experience by teaching a course.

During 2015-16, she took the unusual step of charting her own academic path and created her own personal research sabbatical. Self-sponsored, Maria Paz Esguerra was building her research portfolio while taking the time to experiment and reflect on just what makes higher education meaningful to her. Building on the years preceding it, she used the year to acquire the credentials needed to have a successful faculty career in the future. She acknowledged that it is a big risk to go without a formal institutional affiliation for a year, but for her it was a carefully calculated one.

During her personal sabbatical, she made new discoveries...deliberately. Her interview follows:

> This year has brought both personal and professional growth. I have the ability to make choices and create my own path free of any constraints set by a tenure clock. I have learned that research and service are very meaningful to me.... I have seen other possibilities emerge—even positions outside academia. I have found that all of my academic skills are transferable; I am just using those tools differently. Every day I am engaging in problem solving, in group projects. Research used to be an isolating endeavor, now I have a "writing accountability" partner providing social and writing support. I also take advantage of online writing support such as webinars where writers and editors work together.

> Taking the risk to leave academia meant that I also needed to take on something else in terms of service. I started volunteering for the Greater Baltimore Urban League's college readiness program, and through it I feel committed to social justice in a way that feels genuine and productive. I want to be able to continue to experience these moments for the rest of my career. So I know that I will still need to find time to volunteer for a cause I really care about, that can really

rejuvenate me and provide another opportunity for self-exploration. If I were to advise others, I would say they should select a service activity that is true to the person they are and reflects a cause they feel passionately about.

My academic writing is a much more pleasant experience now. I am able to give my full attention to it and get reconnected to my research. And by being fully engaged, I realize just how much I love it. The personal sabbatical has created the type of nurturing environment I know will produce my best work. I intend to keep on intentionally creating the mental spaces so that I can devote undivided attention to my research.

My biggest initial challenge is that as a personal sabbatical with no institutional affiliation, there was not a predetermined structure of expectations nor an established academic community. I have had to create both, but I miss the real structure and the real sense of academic community.

It is definitely a risk to take a nonstandard path, but I believe I have discovered my path towards health and happiness in higher education. It is an academic life that includes a non-academic network. For me, that is the meaningful path rather than the prestigious path.

Questions for Reflection

1. Which activities do you consider non-urgent and important?

2. How do you avoid non-urgent and unimportant activities?

3. What are three SMART goals (specific, meaningful, achievable, reflected upon, and time-bound) that you have related to self-perseverance?

4. The types of thoughts that lead to stress are repeated and negative; they are called ANTS (automatic negative thoughts). Do you think that everyone has ANTS? Why do you think that some people let the ANTS control their lives and others are more in control of their ANTS?

5. What are three ways to improve your work–life balance?

6. In what ways do you incorporate some of the relaxation strategies in your work–life balance? What relaxation strategies that were not mentioned in the chapter would you like to incorporate in your life?

7. How are mental and physical wellbeing connected to self-care?

8. If you had to transfer your skills, education, and qualifications to a profession outside higher education, which profession would you select?

9. If you had to write mission and vision statements for your life, what would they be?

10. What things can your institution do to promote self-care?

My Higher Education Journal

Please use this space to respond and reflect on the ideas presented in this chapter for your own professional growth.

References

Bandura, A. (1977). Self-efficacy: Toward a unifying theory of behavioral change. *Psychological Review, 84,* 191-215.

Bandura, A. (1982). Self-efficacy mechanism in human agency. *American Psychologist, 37,* 122-147.

Bourne, E. (2015). *The anxiety and phobia workbook (6th ed.).* Oakland, CA: New Harbinger Publications.

Constandse, R. (n.d.) Writing a personal mission statement. *Time thoughts: Resources for personal and career success.* Retrieved from http://www.timethoughts.com/goalsetting/mission-statements.htm

Covey, S. R. (1989). *The 7 habits of highly effective people.* New York, NY: Simon & Schuster.

Dweck, C. (2000). *Self-theories: Their role in motivation, personality, and development.* Philadelphia, PA: Psychological Press.

Fullan, M. (2013). *Stratosphere: Integrating technology, pedagogy, and change knowledge.* Don Mills, Ont.: Pearson.

Henry, A. (2014). *Productivity 101: A primer to the Pomodoro technique.* Retrieved from https://lifehacker.com/productivity-101-a-primer-to-the-pomodoro-technique-1598992730

Hu, S., & Kuh, G. D. (2001, April 10-14). "Being (dis)engaged in educationally purposeful activities: The influences of student and institutional characteristics." Paper presented at the American Educational Research Association Annual Conference. Seattle, WA.

Kezar, A., & Kinzie, J. (2006). Examining the ways institutions create student engagement: The role of mission. *Journal of College Student Development, 47(2),* 149-172.

Kuh, G. D., Kinzie, J., Schuh, J. H., & Whitt, E. J. (2005). Never let it rest: Lessons about student success from high-performing colleges and universities. *Change: The Magazine of Higher Learning, 37(4),* 44-51.

Parkinson, Cyril N. (19 November 1955*).* Parkinson's Law. *The Economist.* London.

Yeager, D. S., & Walton, G. M. (2011). Social-psychological interventions in education: They're not magic. *Review of Educational Research,* 81, 267–301. doi:10.3102/0034654311405999